2 1765 0006 8265 1

T3-BSF-902

WITHDRAWN

GARLAND PUBLICATIONS IN COMPARATIVE LITERATURE

FORSYTH LIBRARY
FORT HAYS STATE UNIVERSITY

General Editor
JAMES J. WILHELM
Rutgers University

Associate Editors
DANIEL JAVITCH, New York University
STUART Y. MCDOUGAL, University of Michigan
RICHARD SÁEZ, The College of Staten Island/CUNY
RICHARD SIEBURTH, New York University

A GARLAND SERIES

ALLEN G. WOOD

LITERARY SATIRE AND THEORY

A Study of Horace, Boileau, and Pope

GARLAND PUBLISHING, INC.
NEW YORK & LONDON
1985

© 1985 by Allen G. Wood

All Rights Reserved

Library of Congress Cataloging in Publication Data

Wood, Allen G., 1950–
Literary satire and theory.

(Garland publications in comparative literature)
Bibliography: p.
1. Verse satire—History and criticism. 2. Poetics.
3. Horace—Humor, satire, etc. 4. Horace—Knowledge—Literature. 5. Boileau Despréaux, Nicholas, 1637–1711—Humor, satire, etc. 6. Boileau Despréaux, Nicholas, 1637–1711—Knowledge—Literature. 7. Pope, Alexander, 1688–1744—Humor, satire, etc. 8. Pope, Alexander, 1688–1744—Knowledge—Literature. I. Title. II. Series.
PN1435.W6 1985 809.1'7 84-48360
ISBN 0-8240-6715-0 (alk. paper)

The volumes in this series are printed on acid-free, 250-year-life paper.

Printed in the United States of America

For Sharon, whose love and support has kept me from becoming a satirist.

CONTENTS

CHAPTER I

INTRODUCTION

Horace, Boileau, and Pope concur in their belief that a poet must limit his literary work to a single area of his greatest strength and knowledge, although their terminology varies from *vis* (force) to *talent* and "science."[1] Because of the theoretical advice these three poets give, we should expect to find restraint in the choice of genre and subject matter within their own works. And this is the case. Their theoretical poems (Arts of Poetry) delineate poetic procedures and values; basic to their effectiveness is not only the exposition, but also the exemplification, of poetic precepts. It is true that all the poetry of Horace, Boileau, and Pope is highly self-conscious and "literary," a fact evident in the careful crafting and artificial constructing of harmoniously correct lines of verse. Yet many instances occur in which literature itself, the craft of writing poetry, becomes the explicit subject of a poem. These poems are even more overtly self-referential, being poetry about poetry. In this study we will concentrate on the particular instances of self-referential verse in order to establish the unity of generic and thematic approach of Horace, Boileau, and Pope, and to ascertain more clearly the exact nature of their own single *vis*, *talent*, or "science."

The texts may be explicitly self-referential in two ways: they may either have literature in general, or the poet's own literature, as their subject matter. Keeping in mind the general or personal focus, we see that the works of Horace, Boileau, and Pope converge on two forms of literature: the poems of literary theory (their Arts of Poetry) and the satires on literary topics (their "literary satires").

To avoid ambiguity, we need to clarify the term "literary" satire. It can be used to refer to "written" satire, contrasted with "visual" or "oral" satire, as suggested in Kernan's The Plot of Satire:

> The attempt to balance the positive and negative forces of oral satire led to the creation of new types of literary satire and to the emergence of the form as "art."[2]

Because all the satire to be examined in our study is written, the frequent connotation of "literary" satire meaning "written" satire need not distract us from its main significance -- which is to refer to the subject matter of the satires and not their method of communication. "Literary" satire describes those works of satire which take an aspect of literature (not politics, religion, marriage) as their subject. It is this second connotation of the term that C. O. Brink emphasizes in his criticism on Horace:

> The Ars Poetica agrees with the literary Satires in its personal and contemporary complexion; in spite of the Aristotelian and Neoptolemic provenance of its basic thought, no one but Horace could have written the work ....[3]

Starting even before Horace, literary satire has a lengthy and rich tradition, which has not received proper attention from modern critics, the inheritors of this critical-satiric discourse.[4] One aim of this study will be to explore literary satire with particular reference to its conection to the poetry of literary theory in Horace, Boileau, and Pope. The two forms, as treated by these three poets, have not been comprehensively analyzed for structural similarities.[5]

The formal verse satires are generically comparable in all three poets, to the greatest extent possible for any three poets in the long tradition of literary satire. We will focus our attention on the following verse satires: Horace's Sermones 1.4, 1.10, 2.1; Boileau's Satires II, VII,

IX; and Pope's "Epistle to Dr. Arbuthnot," "To Mr. Fortescue," and the "Epilogue to the Satires." The theoretical poems to be considered are, of course, Horace's *Ars poetica,* Boileau's *Art poétique*, and Pope's *Essay on Criticism*.

Indeed, these three poets are particularly good representatives not only of literary satirists, but also of literary critics. In the history of literary criticism they provide a striking example of diversity within a unified, consistent viewpoint. The lines of influence are strong; both Boileau and Pope wanted to *be*, in effect, the Horace for their own time and country.[6] As for Boileau:

> Un surnom traditionnel fait de Boileau l'Horace français ...[7]

> A traditional nickname calls Boileau the French Horace.

He helped foster this opinion himself by such statements as the following comment in *Satire* IX, "A Son Esprit":

> Vous vous flattez peut-être en votre vanité:
> D'aller comme un Horace à l'immortalité:....[8]

> You flatter yourself, perhaps out of vanity,
> To proceed, like Horace, toward immortality.

As for Pope, his goal of emulating the Roman satirist was just as fixed:

> Throughout his work Horace was often his model, consciously so, if not, as in the *Imitations*, avowedly so:
> Let me be Horace, and be Ovid you.[9]

Because they achieved their goal to be a new Horace, rather than to be like the historical model, both Boileau and Pope attained a great degree of originality in poetic construction and rhetorical strategy while fulfilling the role of the Horatian poet-censor for their period. Many controlling factors limit the variables of such protean forms as literary satire and the poems of literary theory. We will consider the similarities which unify the literary satires and the Arts of Poetry of these three poets.

First, a critical approach is basic to both forms of poetry. We find a hierarchy of values established in the poems, with clearly distinguished poles of good and bad literary practices. A critical approach is revealed both by the judgments themselves, and also by their method of presentation. They are not stated in an objectively analytic style, but a partisan position is taken. The poems originate in the polemical disputes of the author. Furthermore, a critical approach shapes the general context of both forms of poetry. There is a just appraisal of value, with the results (and not the analytical process) presented in statements which only appear objective.

The partisan position of the literary values reveals the intention of the critical approach, which is less to analyze than to move by rhetorical persuasion. The satires and Arts of Poetry are carefully composed for a maximum rhetorical effect; the audience is engaged early in the poems and led to an agreement with the hierarchy of literary values. Persuasion is achieved not by a confrontation of values, nor a real dialectic, but by the sustained, self-validating argument of the poet. No opponents have an opportunity to argue their position effectively, since the poet's voice is the only one in the poem. If values are contrasted, it comes from the two poles of the poet's own hierarchy, and not from an external value system. Yet these poems appear to offer a contrast and to present a dialectic situation of debate; more voices seem to be speaking than just the poet's.

These appearances contribute to the fictional element of the two forms of poetry. We can readily see that only a small degree of fiction informs the works, since we are not taken far from the real world. The "I" of the poems is portrayed much like the poet, and allusions to topical events and contemporary poets often occur. Characters, dialogues, and situations appear to be real, but are actually artificial constructs, carefully selected and arranged for a persuasive effect when transferred to the real-life literary debate. And not only is this minimal fictionality most suitable for the final rhetorical aim of the poems, but it also produces a pleasurable aesthetic effect for the reader. Horace advises:

> ficta voluptatis causa sint proxima veris ....
> (*Ars poetica*, 338)
>
> Fictions meant to please should be close to the real ....

If the end of these forms of poetry is persuasion, the means to that end involve the fictionality of the "I" as a *persona* or mask of the poet, and the naming of other poets who function as symbols of poetic values. We will return later in this chapter to discuss the role of the persona, whose fictive identity is a key concept to this entire study. For the moment, it is important to consider the fact that the truthfulness claimed in the poems comprises one of their greatest fictions, serving an essentially rhetorical goal. As Paulson indicates in *The Fictions of Satire*, the rhetorical goal ultimately takes precedence over the fiction:

> To the extent that satire presents, and so represents, its "object," it is related to other mimetic forms. But to the extent that satire attacks, it is rhetorical -- the *vituperatio* of *laus et vituperatio* [praise and blame] -- and there is a persuasive end in sight. However much mimesis or representation is involved, the generic end is rhetorical.[10]

In discussing the "generic end" of both forms of poetry, we need to comment on the *generic interrelationship* which unites them. Although traditionally a satire is distinguished from an epistle in that the first is addressed to a person present in the poem, and denounces a fault, the distinction soon became blurred in actual practice. It is true that the *Arts of Poetry* grew out of the epistle tradition in

Horace, but Boileau's _Art poétique_ is unrelated to his _Epîtres_, and Pope called his theoretical poem an "essay" on criticism. Even more inconsistently, Pope's best known verse satire is called an epistle: the "Epistle to Dr. Arbuthnot." The very fact that the nominal distinctions between these genres soon collapsed indicates a similarity of purpose and unity of design which underlies literary satire and the theoretical poems.

Besides the generic interrelationship, a _tonal connection_ also unites the two forms of poetry. The term "satire" can refer both to the genre of formal verse satire, and also to a satiric tone infiltrating almost any other genre. Similarly, theory can inform an entire poem (the _Arts of Poetry_), or contribute to other forms of literature. In the poems under discussion, a satiric tone occurs in the _Arts of Poetry_, and theoretical passages are found in the satires.

Finally, the poems under consideration all stem from a _classical_ (or _neoclassical_) period. This implies a set standard, a corpus of rules for judging literary values, a framework for our poets' hierarchy of value. Curiously, it is the _Arts of Poetry_ of these poets which are cited as a major repository for the (neo)classical standard of each country, although they are more a collection of commonplaces expressed in a more memorable verse form than theoretical treatises. For example, the principle of dramatic unities is well expressed in Boileau's succinct distich:

> Qu'en un lieu, qu'en un jour, un seul fait accompli
> Tienne jusqu'à la fin le théâtre rempli.
> (_Art poétique_, III, 45-46)
>
> In one place, in a day, a single action completed
> Will keep the theatre full until the play's end.

But one must look elsewhere for the actual theory supporting these generalized conclusions. The theoretical poems provide, then, only a brief summary of the classical rules. As for the literary satires, little direct conection is expressed between them and the standardized rules of judgment. If the Arts of Poetry convey commonplaces rather than analytical theory, the literary judgment in the satires is one step further removed from the commonplaces. In the satires other poets are not satirized specifically for deviating from a poetic norm or rule, such as the dramatic unities, but they are condemned for a general ineffectiveness. As Boileau states:

> Le secret est d'abord de plaire et de toucher:
> Inventez des ressorts qui puissent m'attacher.
> (*Art poétique*, III, 25-26)
>
> The foremost secret is to please and touch:
> Find some mechanism that will hold me.

Accordingly, literary satire proceeds only from the most general, and at the same time the most essential, rule of criticism.

Classicism also implies a general community of authors in a Republic of Letters, functioning as a closely-knit, elite subculture serving society by the production of socially useful literature. Both the literary satires and the Arts of Poetry establish an elite community by excluding certain claimants and furnishing guidelines for membership. Because Horace, Boileau, and Pope take a critical approach, they are highly selective in ranking poets and poetic practices in two very different classes. And the concept of "classes" is essential to classicism:

> Dans cette vision hiérarchique de l'art littéraire, le vrai poète, l'auteur "classique", est celui qui se scinde de la foule des "froids écrivains", qui sort du commun, qui se départ du vulgaire, par la *classe* extraordinaire de ses écrits.[11]
>
> In this hierarchical vision of literary art, the true poet, the "classical" author, is the one who breaks from the crowd of "dull writers", who distinguishes himself, who rises above the masses by the extraordinary *class* of his writings.

The two classes of poets are distanced on a hierarchical

structure in the most common image of poetic judgment: Mount Parnassus. Appearing in both the literary satires and the Arts of Poetry, the image represents both a unified view of all poets and poetry, while separating the few elite on the top from the mass of poetasters on the bottom. Literary satire focuses down upon the lowlands of Parnassus while the theoretical poems prescribe rules for climbing up to the summit (the mountain's twin peaks). Concerned with the same general topic, their perspectives are radically different. We should now consider the differences between the two forms of poetry.

Both take a critical approach to their subject matter, but the Arts of Poetry offer constructive criticism on achieving excellence while the literary satires ridicule practices deemed reprehensible. Because of this difference in critical approach, arising from the difference in focus on the Parnassian extremes of poetic value, the two forms of poetry lead in separate directions toward different rhetorical ends. The theoretical poems defend an entire aesthetic system by establishing a program of correct poetic practices, whereas the literary satires move the reader to condemn certain poets in defense of an unjustly maligned persona.

To arrive at these different rhetorical goals, the persona in both forms is engaged in a different fictional framework. In the Arts of Poetry, he appears as a master craftsman addressing an apprentice poet on the rules of their craft, with a direction that is fixed in the future. The literary satires, however, portray a heroic persona who triumphs over mass calumny and attack. The temporal direction is oriented toward the past, and the focus is centered on the dynamic process of the poet's life and work. The persona offers himself as an example of a poet struggling against harsh criticism in his climb up Parnassus, whereas in the theoretical poems he withdraws as a poet in order to counsel others on the values which will lead to the summit of Parnassus.

The differences in critical approach, rhetorical goals, and fictional framework which separate these two forms of poetry need to be explored in greater detail. The figure of the persona is readily available for textual analysis, and is centrally implicated in the divergence of methods and aims. Therefore, we will analyze the means by which the literary satires and the poems on literary theory of Horace, Boileau, and Pope establish different fictional frameworks for their differing rhetorical goals, which can be seen by examining the specific uses of the poet's textual presence, or persona.

The concept of a persona illustrates the shift from a historical, biographical reading of satire which considered the narrator, "I," as the poet himself, to a new focus on the text itself and the poet's fictional mask (*persona*). Critical attention was directed to the concept of a satiric persona with Maynard Mack's article "The Muse of Satire," whose title summarizes the article's a-historical position:

> I have ventured in my title to name the Muse. For the Muse ought always to be our reminder that it is not the author as man who casts these shadows on our printed page, but the author as poet ....[12]

The functions of the terms "Muse" and "persona" underscore the element of fictionality in satire, a fictionality that can easily be overlooked because of its closeness to reality.

The split between persona and author is most noticeable in formal verse satire when an inconsistency appears between the poet's supposed beliefs (revealed in correspondence, diaries, or reported discussions) and those of his poetic persona. Inconsistencies also may develop between personae of a poet's different poems. We will examine the plausible relationship between the poet and his persona in the next chapter when we explore the fictional constructs of literary satire. A high level of correlation nonetheless exists between the fiction and the reality it portrays.

The persona often utters or implies favorable opinions held by the poet, and condemns people and practices he wishes criticized. Boileau's persona ridicules Chapelain as author of La Pucelle, and Boileau actually disliked Chapelain. Horace was a protégé of Maecenas, as his satires demonstrate, and Pope loathed Lord Hervey in actuality and in the satires. Thus the persona is not a totally fictive creation, divorced from the poet (as may occur in epic or drama). Ehrenpreis' article "Personae" emphasizes the realistic content of satire, and counterbalances Mack's concept of a fictive persona. A synthesis of the two critical positions provides a focus on the poetic "I" as an intermediary, showing satire to present both reality and fictionality:

> ...the satirist structures an artifice at the same time that he offers a certain kind of self-revelation.[13]

Ambiguity resulting from this simultaneous masking and revealing requires a shifting of positions within a poem and among poems, so that the "truth" of the satirist may seem like hypocrisy if the device of the persona is not kept in mind. As the satirist Charles Churchill remarked about an anonymous poet:

> Ev'ry one who knows this author, knows
> He shifts his stile much oft'ner than his
> cloaths.[14]

The satirist himself "shifts clothes" to create a persona in each new poem; this shifting is one of the basic devices and conventions of the two forms of poetry to be studied.

The different functions which the persona serves will allow us to analyze the different fictional frameworks and rhetorical ends of the two forms. As part of this analysis, the next chapter will explore the fictionality of the persona, addressee, and other poets from the point of view of verisimilitude. Neither form establishes elaborate fictions, nor do literary satires and Arts of Poetry represent actual dialogues. Although claiming to be truthful, these forms present a fictional construct close to historical accuracy. In order to arrive at a better understanding of an a-historical reading of these texts, we will focus on the element of verisimilitude in Pope's "Epistle to Dr. Arbuthnot" and in Boileau's Satire IX, both of which have been prominent in recent criticism of satire as a fictional artifice.

Focusing on the literary satires, the third chapter will examine the structure of the fictional plot which organizes the situations and characters in these satires. Two literary satires will be examined comprehensively in order to demonstrate the basic stages in the movement of the plot, similar for all satires considered in this study. I have chosen Horace's Sermo 1.4 and Boileau's Satire VII because of the diversity of technique and surface disparity which seems to separate them; yet on a deeper level of motivation and character interaction they both reveal the same plot structure. In the fourth chapter a basic morphology of this plot will be described, with the most frequent and fundamental topics analyzed as the basic building blocks of the satiric plot.

The fifth chapter will examine the reason for the shape of the plot, which involves the fictional role of the persona, its relation to the author, and the rhetorical goal of the literary satire. In contrast, the rhetorical goal of an Art of Poetry requires different fictional roles for the persona and the addressee which preclude the formation of a plot, although some of the topics examined in chapter four have analogues in the theoretical poems. The rest of the chapter is devoted to the examination of these analogous topics in the plotless structure of the Arts of Poetry.

The difference between these two forms, revealed through diverse functions of the persona and the different plot structuring of the topics, is also demonstrated by the use of satire in the Arts of Poetry and theory in the literary satires. While the satiric and doctrinal tones of both forms tend to unite them, the difference in frequency and approach reveals the two directions that these forms take: focusing on the bottom and the top of Mount Parnassus. Finally, in the last chapter we will analyze this allegory of Mount Parnassus and the entire mythological representation of the process of writing as portrayed in both forms of poetry. Parnassus is a symbol representing effort and inspiration, both success and failure of the distinct classes of writers, and both the process and the goal of writing itself. In the two forms of self-referential literature, it is the ultimate destination.

By analyzing the two forms in the way just outlined, we will arrive at a better understanding of the essential fictional construct and rhetorical intent of each form, as well as establish a clear basis for distinguishing them on formal and structural grounds. This aspect of the poems has been neglected in previous studies. Because the fictional construct of each form involves a detailed analysis of the poets' personae, we will see how each poet places himself in his poetry and the relationship he builds with his enemies, his addressee, and finally with the readers. For we, too, are drawn into the fictive world and the persuasive intent of the literary satires and theoretical poems of Horace, Boileau, and Pope.

CHAPTER II

LITERARY SATIRE AND VERISIMILITUDE

veris falsa remiscet
Ars, 151

he blends the false with the true

In poetry the false, or at least the feigned, is mixed with the truth of sentiment and situation to create a fictive, pleasing content. In order to understand better the fictive content of literary satire and the concept of *vraisemblance* (verisimilitude, plausibility), the link between the "false" world of art and the "true" world of reality, needs to be further explored. It represents the appearance of truth and reality in a non-realistic context. Although the satirist frequently claims to express a truthful content:

> Truth guards the poet, sanctifies the line
> And makes immortal verse as mean as mine.[1]

and to represent an actual conversation by the dialogue structure of the poem, the relationship between the world of the text and the actual world of the poet is that of plausibility and not actuality.

Inconsistencies between the real world and the satiric poem, or between different texts, offer valuable clues in revealing the artificial nature of these works and their relationship with the poet. It is difficult to find these clues, because such a high degree of factual correlation exists between the texts and the poet's life. In fact, criticism once regarded satire as a highly autobiographical form of literature, making little distinction between the poet and the textual narrator "I". Satiric texts were read like correspondence and diaries, in order to find the poet's true opinions. This former practice of criticism is understandable, however, when we consider the evasive and subtle nature of the fiction in the satires. As Mack states:

> ...the fictionality takes subtler forms and resides in places where, under the influence of romantic theories of poetry as the spontaneous overflow of powerful emotions, we have become unaccustomed to attend to it.
> ("Muse," p. 84)

We should not expect to find great differences between the texts and the stated beliefs of Horace, Boileau, and Pope, since their satire does not provide the ironical or exotic fictions of a Swift or Montesquieu. But the satires of our three poets contain carefully constructed characters, fashioned by each poet. And the most important of these characters is the satirist himself, the poet's persona.

In the case of Horace it is extremely difficult to find inconsistencies between the poet and his personae. Virtually nothing has survived except for the texts themselves; no diaries or letters provide a different perspective to the satires. Furthermore, no significant inconsistencies exist among the personae of his literary satires. We can see, however, that certain poets mentioned have a fictive status. The name "Crispinus" may have referred indirectly to a real poet, but it is used as a fictional cover. Also, in _Sermo_ 1.4, "Fannius" is a fictive name. For purposes of ridicule Horace used pseudonyms, while he named directly poets he wanted to commend: Eupolis, Cratinus, and Aristophanes. Because of the mixture of real and fictive names, the status of the poets mentioned in Horace's _Sermones_ becomes more subtly nuanced between a fictional and a realistic world.

With Pope, much of his work is pertinent. Mack argues that:

> ...we overlook what is most essential if we overlook the distinction between the historical

Alexander Pope and the dramatic Alexander Pope who speaks [the poems]. ("Muse," p. 83)

By examining closely the works of Pope and comparing them both with his life and with each other, we will be able to make the distinction which Mack suggests. One glaring inconsistency between poet and persona occurs in the first dialogue of the "Epilogue to the Satires." Responding to the suggestion of his *adversarius* (addressee) that he quit writing satire, the persona "P." concedes:

> Dear Sir, forgive the prejudice of youth!
> Adieu distinction, satire, warmth, and truth!
> (63-64)

Yet when this satire was written, the "youthful" Pope was actually fifty. The fictional aspect of the persona is thus apparent.

In general, the persona allows the poet freedom to portray himself to the best aesthetic and persuasive advantage, and we can appreciate with Mack the three possible voices of a persona. He may speak as a plain living *vir bonus* (man of honor), a simple hearted *naïf*, or a righteously indignant public defender. Pope shared qualities with the textual voices of the *vir bonus* and public defender, but he was not a *naïf*. One of the most self-conscious and diligent craftsmen in English poetry created a persona who was amazed at his own involvement in literature. "I lisp'd in Numbers, for the Numbers came" he explains in "Arbuthnot," and he offers a very simplistic, self-effacing reason for continuing:

> I nod in Company, I wake at Night
> Fools rush into my Head, and so I write:....
> ("Fortescue," 13-14)

By projecting himself into his poetry as a persona, Pope also created an idealized self-portrait. The persona represents a highly selective process of characterization:

> The ideal figure, the created poet-persona, who exemplifies the power of virtue in an age of corruption, belongs to the same conception as the

> figure of the eccentric private man with physical infirmities, personal idiosyncracies, and "real personality." ... The figure of the poet, in his heroic aspect, is indeed more type than man, more passion than type.[2]

If the persona occasionally plays a heroic role, then other poets play the villain.

As was the case with Horace, the bad poets ridiculed in Pope's satires are given pseudonyms. In the "Epistle to Dr. Arbuthnot," detailed portrayals of three poets use fictional names. Lord Hervey is criticized most severely of all under the name "Sporus:"

> A. What? that thing of silk
> Sporus, that mere white curd of ass's milk.
> (305-06)

Such veiled references are so numerous in Pope's satires that "keys" to translating the names were often prepared and published, usually by those being satirized.

Pope uses another method to distance the names of poets from reality, although it is less frequent than the pseudonyms. Following Dryden's example of calling Shadwell "Sh---" in "MacFlecknoe" (with scatological implications), Pope refers to poets by incomplete spellings of their real names. The technique is transparent and few Augustan readers could be fooled, yet the truncated names allow a freedom of multiple references that is more characteristic of fiction than documentary prose. In the "Epilogue to the Satires" we are bombarded with partial names:

> The gracious dew of pulpit eloquence,
> And all the well-whipt cream of courtly sense,
> That first was H---vy's, F---'s next, and then
> The S---'s, and then H---vy's once again.
> ("Dialogue I," 69-72)

Finally, the fictionality of the names involves literary convention and intertextual allusions. Horace's "Fannius" is suggested in the name "Lord Fanny" in the satire "To Fortescue". No actual poet is known to be the referent for Lord

Fanny; he serves rather as a type. The typic, symbolic function of all three oblique methods (pseudonyms, incomplete spellings and intertextual allusions) indicate fictionality in the use of these names. Just as the persona is an idealized figure of the poet, so the covert references to other poets represent symbols of absolute incompetence.[3] They refer beyond specific poets to all bad poets, as Fortescue suggests:

> F. A hundred smart in Timon and in Balaam:
> The fewer still you name, you wound the more:
> Bond is but one, but Harpax is a score.
> (42-44)

By the use of oblique references, Pope is able to make examples of specific poets while criticizing the typical faults of entire groups.[4] This two-fold effect is the greatest advantage of the fictional presentation of other poets' names.

A process similar to Pope's creation of fictional personae and symbolic enemies also operates in Boileau's satires, where the artificial separation between text and reality is even more clear. In his <u>Art poétique</u>, Boileau expresses the popular neoclassical opinion that in the theatre a probable fiction may be preferrable to, and more effective than, a real event:

> Jamais au spectateur n'offrez rien d'incroyable.
> Le vrai peut quelquefois n'être pas vraisemblable.
> (III, 47-48)
>
> Never offer anything unbelievable to a spectator.
> The real truth sometimes does not seem probable.

Yet in speaking of the genre which he himself had practiced primarily for the decade preceding <u>l'Art poétique</u>, Boileau speaks of satire solely in terms of its truthful content:

> L'ardeur de se montrer, et non pas de médire,
> Arma la vérité du vers de la satire.
> (<u>Art</u>, II, 145-46)
>
> The drive to display itself, and not slander,
> Armed the truth with satiric verse.

Despite this insistence on the orientation of satire towards truth, Boileau's actual practice of satire necessitated both an element of aesthetic distance and a moral correction of history achieved by fictionality.[5]

Modern criticism of Boileau has contributed greatly to an a-historical reading of the texts, in support of a satiric persona or mask. Although the terminology varies among Borgerhoff, Brody, and Beugnot, each of them suggest that the *je* ("I") in the Satires is not the real Boileau but a textual construct. In his "Boileau Satirist *animi gratia*," Borgerhoff speaks of a "duplicity" inherent in contradictory passages. He concludes that there must be a certain relativity to the truth conveyed by these satires:

> To put it crudely then ... what Boileau says is both "true" and "not true" at one and the same time.[6]

In Boileau and Longinus, Brody discusses the contradiction between statements in Satires II and VII by a Boileau/pseudo-Boileau polarity. And Beugnot describes a doubling process in the distanced stance of the satirist's persona. Whether speaking of duplicity, a pseudo-Boileau, or doubling, these critics reject a historical, biographical reading of the Satires. To extend Borgerhoff's phrase that what Boileau says is both "true" and "not true" at the same time, it would be useful to consider that what Boileau is is both "true" and "not true" simultaneously. Boileau was not recording his real self, but was creating an artificial and idealized self in the Satires, in the form of a persona.

The satirist's *je* may be seen as a poetic construct, as a sign in an utterance, having only a minimal connection with the historical author Boileau. Benveniste raises the issue of reference in its broad linguistic context in his discussion of pronouns:

> Quelle est donc la "réalité à laquelle se réfère je ou tu? Uniquement une "réalité de discours," qui est chose très singulière. Je ne peut

> être défini qu'en termes de "locution," non en termes d'objets, comme l'est un signe nominal.[7]
>
> What is the "reality to which *I* and *you* refer? Solely a "reality of discourse," which is something quite particular. *I* can be defined only in terms of "locution," not in terms of objects, such as a nominal sign.

In other words, "I" is a fictive persona. It is a linguistic void, a verbal shifter -- an idea which is particularly applicable to textual discourse. The fact that critics have tended traditionally to view Boileau's *je* as autobiographical is in itself a strong indication of the degree of plausibility that exists between persona and author.

In *Satire* IX ("A Son Esprit"), we find the most complex and intriguing portrayal of a persona. Unlike the other satiric dialogues in which the satirist and the addressee are clearly differentiated, engaged in an I-you discourse, *Satire* IX preserves a discursive framework while splitting the persona for a self-reflexive dialectic. The basic situation itself is contrived, artificial -- making little pretense to a real conversation. The first line of the satire establishes the split of the persona into the two participants of the dialogue:

> C'est à vous, mon Esprit, à qui je veux parler.
>
> It is you, dear Mind, with whom I want to talk.

A synecdochic relationship exists between the interlocutors; but the identity of the initial *je* is never explained, nor given a label (such as the *Esprit* has). Indeed, the initial opposition between the *je* (presumably a Boileau-like poet) and his *Esprit* (a satiric impulse) conceals a much more complex relationship, in which each interlocutor conveys more than one identity and wears more than one mask.

In schematic form Boileau's projected self can be shown as divided, with each half concealed by several stances, and with each stance rooted in a different context. The reading of the text consists of a movement from the surface opposition between *je* and the *Esprit* to an understanding of a single satiric persona unifying the entire poem.

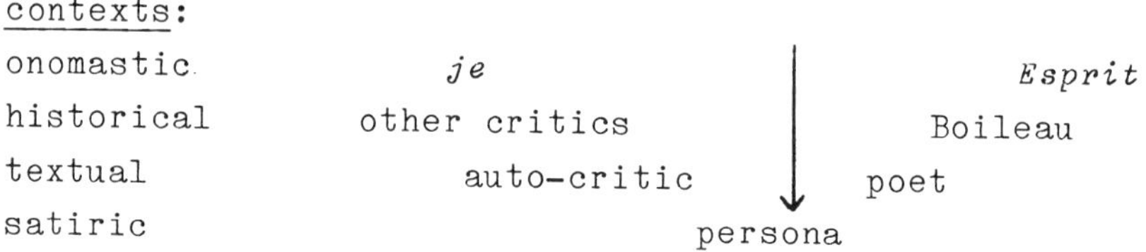

It is the historical context which motivates much of the first half of the satire, since most of the criticism which the *je* levels at the *Esprit* echo real criticisms made of Boileau. The lines:

> On croirait à vous voir dans vos libres caprices,
> Discourir en Caton des vertus et des vices, ...
>
> One would think, seeing you playing whimsically,
> Discoursing like Cato on virtue and vice ...

repeat Cotin's *Critique désintéressée*.[8] Another couplet recalls the anonymous *Instruction à Despréaux*. Yet such charges, taken from the numerous pamphlets that appeared in 1666 and 1667 as part of the quarrel surrounding the publication of Boileau's *Satires* (that is, *Satires* I-VII), are appropriated by the critical *je* of *Satire* IX.

The supposed self-criticism, which subsumes in a selective and simplified manner the complaints of other critics, is a mock-criticism, ironic in tone. In the deep structure, it is the satirist-persona who assumes the mask of a self-critic, in order to defend his poetry and discredit his critics. It is a subtle and complex strategem in which the *je* covers a multi-faceted character. Borgerhoff observes that:

> ...within the framework of the whole imagined situation ... Boileau-censor who, we understand is at least partly a make-believe Boileau, lifts the mask and shows himself to be really Boileau himself, as we know him, after all. (246-47)

It would be better to modify this view. When Boileau-censor lifts his mask, it is not to reveal the "real Boileau," but the more familiar mask of Boileau the satiric persona, the Boileau of the satiric text.

The identity of the *Esprit* presents fewer complexities, although it reveals again the basic structure of a mask covering another mask. The *Esprit*, mental faculty of the poet, reveals the satiric persona himself. Despite the surface opposition between the critical *je* and the *Esprit*, unity is maintained since the satiric persona has really been talking only to himself. By this strategem, the critical conflict is nullified, and the defense of Boileau's satiric practice is assured within its own self-enclosed field of argumentation. This poetic construct impinges upon the world of reality, with a primary thrust coming from the connection between the satiric persona and the historical Boileau.

The element of verisimilitude in the satire is seen in its fictionality. The persona, a reduced and simplified image of Boileau, has textual autonomy. He may state:

> Mais pour Cotin et moi, qui rimons au hasard:...
> Le plus sûr est pour nous de garder le silence.
> (45; 48)
>
> But for Cotin and myself, who rhyme at random:
> The safest is for us to keep quiet.

or question his alter-ego:

> Vous seul plus dégoûté, sans pouvoir, et sans nom,
> Viendrez regler les droits, et l'état d'Apollon?
> (113-14)
>
> You alone, more disgusted, without power or a name,
> Will come to settle the rights, and the realm of
> Apollo?

These are poetically effective utterances, although not accurate as statements of literary history. Given the paradigm of a basic satiric utterance, such as "I satirize Chapelain," the referent for this "I" may appear to be "I, Boileau," but is actually the poetic fiction, the self-referential "I, persona."

The main character, in fact the only character, in Satire IX is the satiric persona, expressed by the verbal shifter *je* in each half of the dialogue. But there are other persons who are named, the victims of satire, whose ontological status should also be examined. The ambiguity of a shifting sign is no longer an issue. For the mention of Cotin, or Chapelain, seems to present an element of reality into the satire. However, the textual characters of the satirized victims are also split. Rather than stating "I, Boileau, satirize Chapelain," the structure of the basic satiric transaction is posited at one remove from this reality, in a realm of minimal fictionality:

> Ma Muse en l'attaquant, charitable et discrète,
> Sait de l'homme d'honneur distinguer le poète.
> (211-12)

> My Muse, charitable and discreet, while attacking him,
> Can distinguish the poet from the gentleman.

Hence, Boileau's Muse (or rather Boileau's persona's Muse) may attack a poet, but Boileau and the particular gentleman are left outside the field of combat.

In addition to this division, there is the implication that the choice of satiric victims is motivated by linguistic needs, by the rules of prosody that govern the material aspect of the names themselves:

> Que vous ont fait Perrin, Bardin, Pradon, Hainaut,
> Colletet, Pelletier, Titreville, Quinaut,
> Dont les noms en cent lieux, placés comme en leur niches
> Vont de vos vers malins remplir les hémistiches?
> (97-100)

> What have they done to you -- Perrin, Bardin, Pradon, Hainaut,
> Colletet, Pelletier, Titreville, Quinaut --
> Whose names, in a hundred spots, are put in their place

> And fill the lines of your wicked poetry?

This linguistic motivation places an emphasis on the signifier of these nominal signs, suggesting that the inclusion of a particular name may be arbitrarily governed by the formal aspects of the signifier as well as by the appropriateness and "truth" of the sign's content, its real-life referent. For Boileau, onomastics exerts a poetic function.

There is another indication that the names of the satirized victims do not correspond directly to their realistic referents. Boileau often changed the names in his public readings of his satires in order to convey his most recent displeasures. Some of these variants figured in the different editions of the _Satires_, documented by Antoine Adam in _Les Premières Satires de Boileau_. Adam notes another arbitrary motivation for the inclusion of names in Boileau's satires:

> Boileau semble lui-même admettre qu'il attaquait parfois au hasard, emporté par sa verve satirique. Il reconnaît qu'il a écrit "contre des poètes qu'il ne connaissait point, et qui ne lui avaient fait ni bien, ni mal."[9]

> Boileau seems to admit himself that he sometimes attacked at random, carried away by his satiric impulse. He realized he had written "against poets he did not know, and who had done him neither good nor harm."

The most unusual example of this kind of unmotivated choice, placed in a satiric context, occurs in a version of _Satire_ I before 1664, where we see an ironic comment on:

> ... cet amas de tant de grands Esprits,
> Un Racine, un Ménage auront les premiers prix.
> (Adam, _Premières_, 163)

> ...among this mass of such great wits,
> A Racine, a Ménage, would take first place.

Racine had only written _Alexandre_, and the two poets had not yet become friends. The name "Racine" is significant here not only for the "error" in the satiric message (when viewed from our historical perspective), but also for the form in which the name appears. The indefinite article, "Un Racine," already places the name on a general level, rather than an individual, historically referential level of discourse. The name "Racine," and indeed every name of satirized victims, is used metaphorically, referring to a type -- the Bad Poet.

Names may be generalized in another way. They are occasionally detached from their historical context, given a diachronic freedom and applied in anachronistic contexts. The abbot Cotin (1604-1682) is released from his historical moorings and sent sailing backward:

> Avant lui Juvenal avait dit en latin
> *Qu'on est assis à l'aise aux sermons de Cotin.*
> (Sat. IX, 129-30)
>
> Before him, Juvenal had said in Latin
> *One can sleep peacefully through the sermons of Cotin.*

and forward:

> Mais je veux que le sort, par un heureux caprice,
> Fasse de vos écrits prospérer la malice,
> Et qu'enfin votre livre, aille au gré de vos voeux,
> Faire siffler Cotin chez nos derniers neveux.
> (Sat. IX, 79-82)
>
> But I hope Fate, by some fluke,
> Causes the malice of your writing to prosper,
> And that your book goes well, as you wish,
> So that Cotin is scorned among our last descendents.

It serves as an example for all times. The names of the satirized victims are, then, self-referential in the context of the satiric (poetic) utterance, just like the *je* of the persona. The names must properly fill a hemistich, and function as a metaphoric sign for the Bad Poet.

Both the subject and object, the two characters of the basic satiric utterance "I, Boileau satirize Chapelain," have been (at least minimally) separated from their strictly realistic referents. The statement now reads: "I, persona, satirize a Chapelain." These two utterances are linked by a connection of plausibility. Yet the verb, describing the whole process of satirizing, must also be re-examined in order to determine whether it conveys a real action or the mere semblance of an action.

Although in the Art poétique Boileau claims a close connection between satire and the truth (II, 145-46), there is no mention made of truth in the three passages of Satire IX that define satire. In accordance with the Horatian metaphor of *ut pictura poesis*, the first description of satire relates it to the contrastive technique of shading:

La satire ne sert qu'à rendre un fat illustre
C'est une ombre au tableau qui lui donne du lustre.
(199-200)

Satire serves only to make a fool better known,
It is a shadow, which emphasizes the picture's
luster.

In this context, satire is described as a method of representation, at one remove from reality; truth does not strictly apply to shadows. The second description is more pragmatic and occupationally oriented: satire is a "métier funeste" (deadly trade). This description, like the first, is negative. The following passage comes closer to explaining what poetic satire actually is:

La satire en leçons, en nouveautés fertile,
Sait seule assaisonner le plaisant et l'utile,
Et d'un vers qu'elle épure aux rayons du bon sens,
Détrompe les Esprits des erreurs de leur temps.
(267-70)

Satire, full of lessons and novelties,
Can alone add spice to the pleasant and useful,
And, with a line it purifies by good sense,
Clarify minds from the errors of their day.

The important word is *leçons*, which denotes the didactic purpose of satire. But the word may also refer to variant textual or factual versions of a truth:

> Il se dit, figurément et familièrement, d'un récit qui diffère d'un autre relatif au même fait. "Vous racontez ainsi l'aventure; mais il y a une autre leçon, une leçon différente."[10]

> It is said, figuratively and ordinarily, of an account that differs from another relative to the same fact. "You relate the adventure thus; but there is another version (reading), a different version.

Hence, a satiric *leçon* may be based on an opinion, and may aim to persuade listeners and readers of its truth by a process of verisimilitude. This is similar to Todorov's notion of different *récits* (accounts) of a real event.[11] With this perspective, we can view Boileau's satires as *leçons*, or personal *récits*, which the audience is persuaded to accept as true. This persuasion is effected by the close plausibility between the language of the text and the real-life situation. The statement "Chapelain is a bad author" is an opinion based on personal taste and subjective norms; yet Satire IX presents this opinion within its own poetic, self-referential construct as an absolute truth:

> Son livre en paraissant dément tous ses flatteurs.
> Ainsi, sans m'accuser, quand tout Paris le joue,
> Qu'il s'en prenne à ses vers que Phébus désavoue,
> Qu'il s'en prenne à sa Muse allemande en français.
> Mais laissons Chapelain pour la dernière fois.
> (238-42)

> His book, when it appears, gives the lie to his flatterers.
> Thus, without accusing myself, when all Paris plays with him,
> Let them attack his lines which Apollo disavows,
> Let them attack his German Muse in French.
> But let's leave Chapelain for the last time.

But the bitter quarrels and polemical pamphleteering that surrounded the publication of Boileau's Satires demonstrate that they were only one *leçon* in a dispute based on taste.

In Satire IX the persona himself, moreover, acknowledges twice that he is relating opinion, not fact:

Mais moi, qui dans le fond sais bien ce que j'en crois

En les blâmant enfin, j'ai dit ce que j'en crois (13; 201)

But as for me, who knows at heart what I believe

By blaming them, finally, I said what I believe

Satire has more to do with *croire* (believing) than *savoir* (knowing), although the former creates a semblance of the latter. In the basic satiric paradigm, the apparent message, "I, Boileau, know that Chapelain is a bad poet" is translated by the textual discourse, "I, persona, believe that a Chapelain is a bad poet." The bridge between these two utterances must be sought in the self-referential language of poetry. The persona places the names of real poets on his own fictive Parnassus of poetic values, claiming truth as he structures a picture of contemporary poetry based on subjective opinion. Subtle distinctions and nuances of experience are removed, so that the characters represent extreme positions. Such simplification also furthers the poet's attempt to rectify the actual situation, to justify himself, and to expose poets he considers bad. In order to achieve this rectification of reality, our literary satirists not only create life-like characters, but they place them in action within a plot structure.

CHAPTER III

THE SATIRIC PLOT

One of the most significant characteristics of the fiction of literary satire is the presence of a basic plot which organizes the content of the satire around the persona and moves toward a conclusion. This not only distinguishes literary satire from the poems of literary criticism, but also differentiates literary satire from other kinds of satire.[1] According to a general view of satire, stated in Kernan's Cankered Muse:

> If we take plot to mean, as it ordinarily does, "what happens," or to put it in a more useful way, a series of events which constitute a change, then the most striking quality of satire is the absence of plot.[2]

The satiric representation of the world depicts contention without resolution, antithesis without synthesis:

> The normal "plot" of satire would then appear to be a stasis in which the two opposing forces, the satirist on one hand and the fools on the other, are locked in their respective attitudes without any possibility of either dialectical movement or the simple triumph of good over evil. ...This constant movement without change forms the basis of satire, and ... creates the tone of pessimism inherent in the genre.
>
> (pp. 31,33)

This is true for satire which focus on matters of religion, politics, or morality. All such objects of satire are separate from both the satirist and the fools satirized. No change can be effected on the object itself.

Literary satire, being self-referential literature, is more tied to the satirist-persona and his practice of writing satire. It presents a more straightforward confrontation between him and his foolish opponents, without an intermediate object of satire. Because the satirist creates the fictional world of the literary satire, the stasis can be broken, and a change can occur to resolve the plot.

Kernan later modified his position in The Plot of Satire, in which he suggests that there are several kinds of plot besides the strict Aristotelian formula. He describes the rising and falling plot movement in Volpone, and the circular patterns in Evelyn Waugh's satiric novels, yet he does not examine individual formal verse satires for a plot progression.[3] Kernan bases his concept of plot upon the action in a work:

> My own position is that any work of literature in which there is action, in which there is a shift of position or scene, in which there is any kind of physical or psychic movement, has a plot.
> (p. 100)

We need to analyze the literary satires for such a plot.

In the satires of Horace, Boileau, and Pope, a three stage development of the plot provides a general movement to the argument. The three stages are not rigorously delineated, but a range of variability within the stages, and a possibility for recurrence of the entire three stage pattern, allow for a great flexibility in the construction of the fictional plot. At the center of these variations lies the basic progression: from threat to response, and a final triumph.

The threat almost always comes from outside the persona, representing an impediment to his continued practice of satire. An external change is proposed, ranging from a threat on the persona's life to a friend's suggesting another genre than satire. In any event, he is not supposed to continue writing as he had previously written. The response occurs when the persona presents himself in the poem, defines his ethical character and poetic practice, and defends himself against the unjust nature of the threat. This is often the crucial intersection of the argument, during which other characters and their threats are diminished, and the role of the persona and his defense are asserted. The threat is shown to be based on faulty assumptions: it is wrong, foolish, or false, while the actual practice of the persona has been correct and necessary.

The threat and response represent the two perspectives that are found in most kinds of static satire, the two sides of the argument. According to the pattern of literary satire, it is unique that the opposing threat is consistently given the opening stage in the argument, and that a third stage to the argument resolves it. The persona triumphs; the unjustified threat will be ignored. The satirist will continue to write as he had written, without any changes, but with personal security and artistic freedom to pursue his career as a satirist. The first two stages portray the satirist's past practices and present danger, while the final stage is future-oriented, moving beyond the usual stasis of satire.

In the nine literary satires to be studied in this chapter, many permutations of this basic three-stage plot structure occur. Horace's _Sermo_ 1.4 moves from an aesthetic threat to an ethical response. _Sermo_ 1.10 begins with a response; the threats are unstated antecedents to the poem. In _Sermo_ 2.1 a double threat from the poet's readers and from his interlocutor Trebatius opens the satire. Yet despite all these threats, the persona triumphs at the conclusion.

The ends of Boileau's satires are slightly problematic, since in all three a self-imposed silence justifies poetic closure. In _Satire_ VII, during the general movement from threat to triumph, a deft interplay of pronouns first conceals, then reveals, the persona. _Satire_ II presents a paradoxical treatment of the satiric plot because the threat, stated by the persona himself, is repeated again at the end of the poem. However, the argument of the poem shows that this threat is really a triumph for the persona, in a satire in which values are given an ironic twist. Finally, in Satire IX the threats are massed in the first half of the poem in the voice of the *je*, while the second half of the poem provides an accumulative response and triumph for the *Esprit*. All three of Boileau's literary satires are self-contained artifacts, cast in dialogue form but without an "outsider" to pose a serious threat.

In contrast, an interlocutor is presented in all three of Pope's literary satires, but his role varies from friend to threatening enemy. In the "Epistle to Dr. Arbuthnot" a series of threat-to-triumph movements ends with a moral triumph, confirmed by the poet's friend Arbuthnot. In "To Mr. Fortescue" (Imitations of Horace), the same basic pattern as in Horace's Sermo 2.1 is preserved, with initial threats from both readers and the lawyer-interlocutor. But in the end, the persona's lawyer assures him of a legal victory. In "Dialogue I" in the "Epilogue to the Satires," the interlocutor is the source of the threats, within a plot structure that ends in an aesthetic triumph (but moral defeat) for the satirist. The triumph of Vices at the end of the satire marks the failure of the poet as a moral reformer -- yet he will continue to write.

Rather than explore all the variations on the basic satiric plot, two satires will be studied in order to show the progression of plot. After this progression has been established, the next chapter will focus on each of the three stages, outlining the typical kinds of threats, responses, and triumphs.

The two satires that will be examined are Horace's Sermo 1.4 and Boileau's Satire VII. The Latin satire is most notable for strong characterizations and a quasi-dramatic presentation of situations, while Boileau's satire is a meditation which progresses by shifts of pronouns. Their different styles provide a great range of variation on the basic structure of the satiric plot, showing the innovative techniques that each satirist brought to the writing of his poems.

Written in approximately 35 B.C. as one of the first works of the young poet, *Sermo* 1.4 is Horace's first satire on a literary topic, and the most complete exposition of his theory of literature until the *Ars poetica* some two decades later. The basic structure of this satire has been identified as bipartite, moving from the aesthetic nature of satire (and poetry in general) to its moral justification.[4] The plot structure supports the division of the poem, progressing from an aesthetic threat and response, interrupted by a moral threat-response-triumph. The final triumph closes the poem and blends the two topics of aesthetics and ethics in a concluding synthesis, a personal and strong victory for the persona which recalls the historical example of the satire's opening lines.

In the beginning, a description of the Golden Age of Old Comedy, set off from the dynamic interchange of the rest of the satire, serves as a touchstone for the rest of the poem:

> EUPOLIS atque Cratinus Aristophanesque poetae,
> atque alii quorum comoedia prisca virorum est,
> si quis erat dignus describi quod malus ac fur,
> quod moechus foret aut sicarius aut alioqui
> famosus, multa cum libertate notabant.
> (1-5)

> Eupolis and Cratinus and Aristophanes, true poets,
> and the other good men to whom Old Comedy belongs,
> if there was anyone deserving to be drawn as a
> rogue and thief,
> as a rake or cut-throat, or as scandalous in any
> other way,
> they set their mark upon him with great freedom.

The status of these writers is established; they are *poetae* whose example is worthy to follow, especially for a young satirist. In the writing of the masters, a general moral threat to society is posed by the man who is *malus* (evil), but the poets respond and "brand" him in a triumph of freedom. The passage does not concern literary satire, but provides instead a conceptual orientation for the satire.

The first threat comes from Crispinus, who has no regard for the persona's privacy nor for good writing. After the Greek satirists and Lucilius have been described, Crispinus cuts short the persona's preoccupation with the past and surges insistently onto the scene. The persona can only interject a quick *ecce* (behold) before Crispinus assumes control and challenges him to a speed-writing contest. For the Horatian persona, quality (not mere quantity) distinguishes excellence in poetry; the *plus scribere* (to write more) of Crispinus' challenge is contrasted by the preceding verse which clarifies the notion of writing as *scribendi recte* (writing correctly). No response is needed to establish that correctness is an essential component of writing, or that poetry is not a contest. Only a bad poet could win such a contest; the persona's apparent defect (judged from Crispinus' values) is an actual asset.

The main threat posed by Crispinus is diminished most significantly by the satiric passage comparing his discourse to the wind: "conclusas hiricinis follibus auras" (like air shut up in goat-skin bellows). He is laughed off the scene, disappearing as the ridiculous figure of Fannius appears. He is presented less as a threat than as a contrastive figure, whose acceptance by the masses is diametrically opposed to the rejection of the persona. Fannius is a crowd-pleaser whose success is measured not by a speed-writing contest, but by more material objects: "Beatus Fannius ultro / delatis capsis et imagine ..." (Happy fellow, Fannius, who has delivered [received] books and a bust). The ablative absolute construction is ambiguous; he may be giving or receiving gifts. An exchange, however, occurs between him and the public, and the statement (especially the *beatus*) is meant to be ironic.

The reading public, the *vulgus* (crowd), presents the main source of the threat in the first half of the satire. The poet can easily ridicule his competitors, but he must maintain a reading public. However, the persona claims to have none because of the nature of his poetry. It is precisely because the masses are the object of satire that they hate writers of satire, "omnes hi metuunt versus, odere poetas" (All of them dread verses and detest the poet, 33). The persona responds, not with a counter-attack, but with a gentle suggestion to explore the facts: "Agedum, pauca accipe contra" (Come now, listen to a few words in opposition, 38). The phrase is the pivotal point of the poem, marking the transition from threat to response, as the persona gains control of the direction of the satire. Other threats emerge, but they are contained directly within the persona's own discourse, rather than dominating the scene like Crispinus and the *vulgus* in the first forty lines.

The persona claims to offer only a few words (*pauca*) in opposition. This modesty is reminiscent of his response to Crispinus, in which he explains that he writes very little (*perpauca*). The persona not only consistently extends his earlier response, but shows through his rhetoric that the threat of the masses is based on a false judgment when applied to his particular poetry. The validity of the statements opposing the crowd to the persona hinges on the ethos of the speaker; the humble response of "Agedum pauca accipe contra" is contrasted to the extravagent rhetoric in the charges against the poets (34-38). Furthermore, a context is already established for each speaker. The persona is favored by the gods, is gentle in his criticism, and a successor to the Greek masters (Eupolis ...). In contrast, the crowd is driven by immorality (26-32). Given the triumph of the poets over immorality in the opening passage, and the description of the persona's ethos as he faced the early threats, the structural shift to a response is consistent and rhetorically valid. At this point the persona has more power to persuade the reader.

The call for a response is successful, and the actual response follows. The main defense which the persona makes throughout the poem is to distinguish himself from both bad poets and the crowd. He does not respond to the hatred of the crowd, but explains his own position in this controversy as being outside the category of *poeta*:

> primum ego me illorum dederim quibus esse poetas
> excerpam numero: neque enim concludere versum
> dixeris esse satis; neque si qui scribat uti nos
> sermoni propiora, putes hunc esse poetam.
> (39-42)
>
> First, I will take my name from the list of such
> as I would allow to be poets.
> For you would not call it enough to round off a
> verse,
> Nor would you count anyone poet who writes, as I,
> Lines more akin to prose.

Consistent with his modest claims, this description of his writing justifies an evasion of the entire issue; the masses hate poets, but he is not one. That is, he is no mere rhymester, for his conception of poetry, real poetry, includes a moral substance. This kind of poetry is given a dignified status.

Just as Crispinus was instrumental in introducing the initial aesthetic threat, so the characters Sulcius and Caprius anticipate the second threat to the persona, one which is ethically oriented. These libelers pose a general threat to society, and the persona distinguishes himself from their activity. At this point he has established a clear hierarchy of *poema*, *sermo*, *libellus*, placing himself in the middle category and exempting himself from societal displeasure. Claiming not to be a libeler, the persona responds to the potential threat (the charge he is one) by directly addressing his audience. The rhetorical question "cur metuas me?" (why do you fear me?) implies a moral stance. He does not spy on the public like Sulcius or Caprius, offer his *libelli* (little books) for public sale, nor recite poems in public.

The responses clarify the relationship between the persona and his audience, which is definitely unlike that which Fannius has. But whereas the persona had earlier complained that nobody dared to recite his verse, he now emphasizes his own public reticence. No threat is implied, but simply a preference to please a few friends. The reading audience of the *amici* (friends) is opposed to the *vulgus*. Rather than respond to the charge that his verse is depraved, or intentionally malicious, the persona challenges the ethical character of the speaker. Only a friend could utter such a statement with any authority, and only a false friend would utter this kind of statement. The persona, having expressed his commitment to his friends as his sole audience, proclaims false friendship to be the blackest crime ("hic niger est," 85) a true Roman could commit. Not only social ties, but national pride, is involved in this first defense against the charge of malicious verse.

The persona responds to the actual charge by citing examples of malicious comments offered at dinner parties, which contrast sharply to his own simple statements. Yet, ironically, the satirist is more feared than the dinner guest who devastates his friends. The persona promises never to write with malice, wishing to build a relationship of trust. In return for honest, open satire, he asks for greater liberty. The plot enters the third phase: triumph. It is not the *poetae*, but the poet's *pater* (father), who has guided him to moral improvement and liberty. The triumph is primarily ethical, rather than aesthetic; this is consistent with the previous responses which de-emphasized the role of the persona as *poeta* to focus on the ethical nature of his verse.

Whereas in the beginning of the poem the *vulgus* had provided the main threat to the persona's poetic career, in the final section they have lost control. After reviewing their sins and follies, the persona proclaims his moral victory:

> Ex hoc ego sanus ab illis,
> perniciem quaecumque ferunt, mediocribus et quis
> ignoscas vitiis teneor.
> (129-31)

> Thanks to their training,
> I am free from vices which bring disaster, but prey
> To lesser frailties you may excuse.

He can pursue a life of contemplation and improvement. Surely this picture of the persona represents a triumph over Crispinus, the masses, and the anonymous false friend. Not only were their threats and charges proved wrong, but their ethics are denounced.

Having been able to establish his moral credibility, the persona concludes the satire with a return to aesthetics, the means by which his ethics are expressed. He will continue writing, or "playing with his papers" (*illudo chartis*, 139), as he modestly claims. But if he is denied this "little vice," then he himself will threaten his critics:

> cui si concedere nolis,
> multa poetarum veniat manus, auxilio quae
> sit mihi (nam multo plures sumus), ac veluti te
> Iudaeci cogemus in hanc concedere turbam.
> (140-43)

> If you should make no allowance for it,
> Then would a big band of poets come to my aid,
> (For we are the majority), and like the Jews,
> We will compel you to join our throng.

The satire ends with this threat, an ironically comic ending, which not only shows the persona's triumph, but also describes him again as a member of the group of poets.

Throughout the course of the satire the persona has developed as an increasingly more complete character, finally able to declare his moral strengths and vanquish his enemies. This development parallels the basic plot progression. A definite change occurs in the poem, exemplified in the two extremes of Crispinus' threat and the persona's own final "threat". There is no static deadlock of opposing positions, but a resolution. Particularly characteristic of Sermo 1.4 is its highly dramatic presentation; the persona is the central character, with dialogue and setting. The fictional world of the satirist's discourse is given a great amount of realistic detail in order to verify the basic plot of threat to triumph.

Boileau's Satire VII also reveals a consistent and regular exposition of the basic plot of literary satire, while using quite different techniques from Horace. An examination of Boileau's satire will help confirm the basic configuration of the satiric plot, and show it producing a very different kind of poem in surface appearance. Whereas Sermo 1.4 is dramatic, Satire VII is reflective, developed less by the confrontation of different characters than by the persona's consideration of alternatives.

Satire VII presents a grammatical tour de force in which the interplay of pronouns is especially effective in the opening passage. Rather than presenting the initial threat from another character, the persona proposes it for himself, after distance is established away from the *je*. Schematically, the first section of the poem is represented in the following shifts in subject (a cycle away from, and back to, the *je*), outlining the first threat and response:

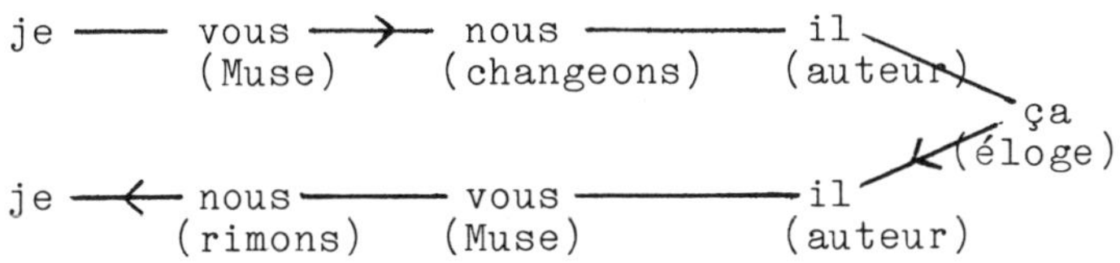

The first line of the satire is rich in implications, "Muse, changeons de style, et quittons la satire" (Muse, let's change our style, and abandon satire). The persona begins with a paradox, a concessive, self-imposed threat. The line contributes to an ironic framing of the satire, which begins on the note of "quittons" and ends with "recommencer" (begin again). Besides this structural paradox, a thematic one exists in the imperative "quittons la satire," initiating a satire. The proposition is obviously, and intentionally, doomed to failure. Yet while it stands, it does represent a concession to the critics of satire. Drastic in its extreme position, it is unparalleled in Horace or Juvenal. Whereas Horace admits he is no *poeta* (of serious genres), and Juvenal promises only to satirize the dead, Boileau's persona proposes the greatest concession possible: silence. He seems to be following the advice of his enemies.

The opening line represents a clear threat to the persona's continued practice of writing satire. But the interplay of the pronouns and the distance already established in the first line are instrumental in creating a fictive context for the proposal. The first word of the poem, "Muse," belies the idea of a traditional invocation. The persona does not seek poetic inspiration, but confers with his own poetic faculty on a proposed change of course. The imperative form of "changeons" and "quittons" further shifts the focus from the singularity of the persona's *je*, and adds complicity to the hypothetical proposition, "Let's change our style." With the imperative forms, a will to change is manifest, without an actual statement that would later be contradicted. Whereas a contradiction may cost the persona his credibility, the abandonment of an unsound and drastic alternative appears very sensible. But first, the threat is further developed.

The basic movement away from the persona continues, and becomes much more impersonal. In the list of charges (2-8), it is unclear where the voice is coming from. The statements represent the basic charges leveled against the satirist by others. But their source is ambiguous; although the persona has internalized the threats against him in this fiction, he does not personally claim agreement. The threats, or critiques of satire, are basically two-fold. Society considers it immoral, and the satirist risks personal safety and professional pride in spreading such immorality. Yet none of the charges are directed especially against the persona, or his own practice of satire, but against the anonymous "auteur" and "poète" of *médisance* (slander). The prospects for the persona to continue writing satire do not seem good at this point, and the justification to "quit satire" appears strong.

The alternative genre of the *éloge* (eulogy) is considered. Although it avoids the charges that threaten satire, charges of public censure and hatred, it faces a different kind of threat. It is dull, and decays rapidly:

> Un éloge ennuyeux, un froid panégyrique,
> Peut pourrir à son aise au fond d'une boutique,
> Ne craint point du public les jugements divers,
> Et n'a pour ennemis que la poudre et les vers.
> (9-12)
>
> A boring eulogy, a cold panegyric,
> Can comfortably rot in a bookstore,
> It does not fear diverse public opinion,
> And for enemies has only dust and worms.

The scene presented is far removed from the human level of discourse and interchange, emphasized by the reified and static book (as opposed to the living word) which awaits the inevitable worm.[5] It is important to notice that in this passage no mention is made of successful eulogy or its effects on poet and public. When the persona later decides to change to the *éloge*, a context for his failure is already provided.

Having reached this point of impersonality with the threat of boredom and future oblivion facing the eulogist, focus is drawn back again to the charges against the satirist. Unlike eulogy, satire has readers, but they often turn on the satirist to become his worst enemies. The reception of satire by the public is paradoxical; whereas Horace's audience hated and feared satiric *poetae*, Boileau's audience is both amused and outraged:

> Et tel en vous lisant admire chaque trait,
> Qui dans le fond de l'âme et vous craint et vous
> hait.
> (19-20)

> And one who reads you and admires each shaft,
> Deep down he both fears and hates you.

The audience's paradoxical reaction is satiric by its very hypocrisy.

The charges that satire is intrinsically bad and poorly received are motivation for the proposal to quit satire -- they provide the main threat of the entire poem. The shift back to this argument on a thematic level is also accomplished on a grammatical level, since the third person of the threatening passages (2-20) is replaced by the structure of discourse established in the opening line. Faced with the hostility of critics and the hypocrisy of the audience, implicitly urging a change, the persona himself suggests a change to his Muse, the only adamant and unshakable satirist in the poem. This seems to be the point of no return. Yet it must be remembered that the proposal is a personally imposed restriction; it can later be lifted by the persona. And the proposal itself must fail, given the earlier context of "boring eulogy."

In fact, the proposal fails immediately and totally.

The first response passage allows the final emergence of the textual *je* (only implied until now). He separates himself from his Muse, and explains his poetic practice, which is the culmination of an intricate and vast interplay of pronouns in the initial passage. The response reveals the persona's total inability to write panegyric. He becomes fragmented into disjointed, resistive parts:

Dès que j'y veux rêver, ma veine est aux abois,
J'ai beau frotter mon front, j'ai beau mordre mes
doigts,
Je ne puis arracher du creux de ma cervelle,
Que des vers plus forcés que ceux de la Pucelle.
Je pense être à la gêne, et pour un tel dessein,
La plume et le papier résistent à ma main.
(27-32)

As soon as I think of it, my inspiration is hard
pressed,
In vain I rub my forehead, bite my nails;
I can drag from the depths of my brain
Only such forced verse as that in the Pucelle.
I think I am being tortured, and for such a task
The pen and paper hold out against my hand.

In order to avoid this torture, and ultimate silence, the proposed alternative must be rejected. The persona will then be free to follow his natural penchant for satire.

By writing satire, the persona triumphs over the threat of silence. Satire is no longer considered bad from a societal viewpoint, but as necessary and good from a personal perspective. It provides the persona material for poetry. In addition, his identity as a poet and the aid of Apollo himself are contingent upon his continued career as a satirist:

Mais quand il faut railler, j'ai ce que je
souhaite;
Alors, certes alors, je me connais poète;
Phébus, dès que je parle, est prêt à m'exaucer,
Mes mots viennent sans peine et courent se placer.
(33-36)

But when I have to mock, I have all I need;
It's then, indeed, I know I'm a poet;

Apollo, as soon as I speak, is ready to comply,
My words come without effort, and run for a place.

This is a triumph of unity and naturalness; the writing of satire places the persona in a state of harmony with himself and with his work. No longer do parts of his body, or the tools of his trade, rebel. The ease of finding fools to satirize and the resulting torrents of verse are recognized by the persona as his triumph over criticism, restriction, and silence:

Aussitôt je triomphe, et ma Muse en secret,
S'estime et s'applaudit du beau coup qu'elle a
fait.
(47-48)

Immediately I triumph, and my Muse in secret
Feels proud, and congratulates itself on a well
placed blow.

At this point, the basic progression from threat to triumph has been achieved.

But while the first half of the poem focused primarily on the threats that impeded the satirist, the second half contains further responses that justify the satirist and build toward a final statement of poetic and satiric liberty. The external, societal distrust of the satirist was not dispelled in the first half of the poem. Having established his aesthetic liberty and regained his flow of verse in the first half, the persona builds his ethical character in the second. Although the situations and motives are different, this is also the Horatian order in Sermo 1.4 for achieving aesthetic liberty and ethical respect.

In the midst of his satiric triumph, the persona reflects that his intention is not to satirize everybody; he responds to the charge that satire is only *médisance* (slander). With the image of the *étamine* (filter), the persona establishes himself as a discriminating moralist, not a mere railer against all mankind.[6] Yet, granted he has a fair judgment, it is not always apparent because of the enthusiasm with which he hounds his satiric victims.

Boileau's persona does not occupy the bottom category of *médisance*, nor is he a true poet (we are reminded of Horace's distinctions *libellus*, *sermo*, and *poema*). In Satire VII, a modest self-evaluation is also evident:

> Enfin sans perdre temps en de si vains propos,
> Je sais coudre une rime au bout de quelques mots:
> Souvent j'habille en vers une maligne prose:
> C'est par là que je vaux, si je vaux quelque chose.
> (59-62)

> Finally, without wasting time with such idle stuff,
> I can stitch together a rhyme after a few words:
> I often dress sharp prose in verse,
> That's what I excel at, if I excel at anything.

The strength of the satirist seems to lie in the formal excellence of versification, expressed by the colloquial verbs *coudre* (stitching) and *habiller* (dressing). The unassuming modesty of the lines contributes to the favorable characterization of the persona, in response to an earlier charge that a satirist is always "seeking honor"(6).

As an interruption to the general portrait of the persona, one final threat is exposed: the threat of death. Potentialy the greatest of all, its delayed appearance (the middle of the poem) places it in a context where it can best be overcome. An extension of the earlier charge that "le mal qu'on dit d'autrui ne produit que du mal" (the ill one speaks of others only produces harm, 4), this death threat maintains the motivation for the persona to describe his moral character and the innocence of his poetic practice. The examples of Lucilius, Horace, and Juvenal are cited as satirists who did not meet a tragic end. And, on a more current and personal level, the persona claims anonymity before the masses. Since he is virtually unknown, the persona has nothing to fear from such a threat:

> Et que craindre, après tout, d'une fureur si vaine?
> Personne ne connaît ni mon nom ni ma veine. (81-82)

> And what should I fear, after all, from idle rage?
> Nobody knows either my name or my style.

Nothing of his has yet been printed, and he is diffident to recite his poems even to his friends.[7] The persona faces nothing harsher than a friendly ridicule for his work.

Having minimized the threat by an exposition of his own practice as a poet, the persona makes his final statement of liberty and moves beyond the dialectic of challenge and response. His vow to continue writing satire follows logically from his responses. Like Horace playing with his papers (*illudo chartis*), Boileau's persona also ends by describing writing as a pleasure (*plaisir*, 89). It is through volition that the persona in this satire triumphs, in contrast to the Horatian persona who more definitely claims a future of writing. Since Boileau's satire is an internal monologue, it is fitting that volition take precedence over action.

In a curious juxtaposition with the concept of volition, which implies internal purpose and control, the final liberty of the persona is expressed as a surrender to the flood of satiric verse that awaits him. In other words, he is active in his choice of genre, but passive before the torrent of verses that come. One of the recurrent themes of the satire is that satire writes itself (33, 36, 43, 46, 93). Only one thing can hinder the persona, and that is his own physical stamina. This is the rationale that motivates the poem's closure, creating a thematic unity for the entire poem. Structural unity is also provided by the framework of an address to the Muse in the opening and closure. But the end of the poem is not an end to all writing; temporarily delayed by a tired hand, the persona assures his Muse: "Mais demain, Muse, à recommencer" (But tommorrow, Muse, we will begin again). The final word, *recommencer*, is the most positive, most triumphant word of the entire satire.

Boileau's Satire VII, like Horace's Sermo 1.4, provides a clear example of the basic plot progression from threat to response and triumph. Satire VII is most notable for its intricate pattern of shifting pronouns, creating an absence of the persona while the main threats against the satirist and satire are raised. Yet despite the lack of a *je* in the first thirty lines of the poem, the greatest threat comes from the poet's proposal to his Muse to "quit writing satire" due to external compulsion. This capitulation must be reversed before the satirist can continue his work. All of this strategy is, of course, an elaborate game which the poet builds into his fictional encounter wih his critics; despite the extreme position which the persona initially takes, it presents a safe, and easily removed, impediment.

More actual satire fills Boileau's poem, used to illustrate the persona's claim that satiric verse flows effortlessly through him. As with Horace, an ethical claim is made for his verse, expressed by the image of the *étamine* (filter) and the general portraiture of the persona as a *vir bonus*, but Boileau's defense is more focused on aesthetic than ethical issues. The final triumph not only comes with the breaking of the block against satire, seen in the overflow of satiric verse (37-45), but in the volition to continue writing in order to satisfy the poet's personal inclination.

Basic to this final triumph, and the argument which leads to it, is the distinction which the persona makes between other satirists who may indeed follow a *méchant métier* (mean craft) and himself. This distinction is more implicit in Satire VII than in Sermo 1.4 where Horace's persona clearly separates himself from the libelers Caprius and Sulcius. As the French satire unfolds it is clear that the earlier charges against satirists simply do not apply to the specific practice of satire which the persona enunciates. Although not specifically countered, these threatening allegations become meaningless as the persona responds by a self-description and a self-portrayal, building credibility for himself and ignoring his incorrect critics.

It has been convenient and natural in the discussion of Satire VII to compare it to Horace's Sermo 1.4, not only for their similarity in basic plot progression, but also for more specific parallels. Both poems contain the same threat that the audience hates a satirist, and similar responses that the persona excels in his craftsmanship of rhymes (rather than more sublime material) and that he limits his audience to only a few friends. Both poems also express the basic distinction between injurious libel and honest, moral satire.

The similarities show the influence of Horace on Boileau. But more importantly, they represent basic themes of literary satire which function effectively in the persuasive fiction of these poems. Because of the vast stylistic and structural differences which separate the two poems, these few similarities gain greater importance as a subtext of the genre of literary satire. Similar threats face the satirist, superseding the boundaries of historical period and nationality. They are limited by the efficacy with which they can be fictionally portrayed and persuasively overcome. This limitation also exists for the kinds of response and the expression of triumph which the persona makes. The similarities and limitations in the threat, response, and triumph of all three poets will be considered in the next chapter.

CHAPTER IV

MORPHOLOGY OF THE PLOT

Boileau recognized the value of his "useful enemies".[1] They provide a reason for writing a response, which leads to a final triumph:

> ...une humeur trop libre, un esprit pou soumis,
> De bonne heure a pourvu d'utiles ennemis:
> Je dois plus a leur haine, il faut que je l'avoue,
> Qu'au faible et vain talent dont la France me loue.
> (Epître VII, 57-60)

> ... a too free humor, a rarely curbed wit,
> Provided, early on, some useful enemies:
> I owe more to their hatred, I must admit,
> Than to my weak talent, which France praises.

Although Horace and Pope did not describe as explicitly as Boileau the elements of a satiric plot in literary satire, it nonetheless exists in their satires.

Rather than continue detailed, intratextual analyses, we will explore the intertextual correspondences among the satires, by making a synchronic study of each stage in the plot progression. We can arrive more quickly at a basic morphology of the plot and perceive the unity which underlies the diverse styles of Horace, Boileau, and Pope. One archetypic literary satire can be derived, which consists of a limited set of variable situations. Although no specific literary satire uses all the elements available at each stage, each satire uses some of them.

The concept of one basic structure provides a significant amount of unity to the works, since the basic message of each poem is similar. Critical attention can be focused on the style of each author, rather than on the content. An examination of each stage allows for an orderly exposition of the traditional topics of literary satire derived from Horace. They are retained by later satirists for their traditional value, as well as their rhetorical effectiveness in persuading an audience. Finally, the basic structure demonstrates clearly that the persona is the central character in literary satire, since it is he who is first threatened, and then responds in order to triumph.

We will first examine the threat. Whereas the response and triumph originate with the persona, the threat comes from an external source, a "useful enemy". He is important to the structure and strategy of each literary satire, providing the stimulus for writing. Without him, the persona would appear to be a railer, since he would be forced into a tactically offensive position. But in the literary satires of Horace, Boileau, and Pope, the enemy is on the offensive, and the persona's defense is made comprehensible, and more modest by the initial threat.

Yet the enemy is rarely presented as a participant in the fictive conversation. Only with the momentary emergence of Crispinus in Horace's Sermo 1.4 does the persona actually face an enemy; none of the addressees is an enemy. Therefore, the threat is controlled and mediated, since it is not directly made but rather reported. Because of the closed environment of the conversation between persona and addressee, the later triumph of the persona is insured.

As the text opens, however, the threat often appears violent and unmanageable. But if the enemy is irrational, it is easier for the persona to portray himself as innocent and credible. Whatever his temperament, the enemy always functions as a blocking character to the persona. He wants to stop the poet from writing satires, which is the one basic threat in the archetypic pattern of literary satire. There are a few ways in which he can stop the persona, either by challenging personal rights, social bonds, or aesthetic beliefs. Each of the three kinds of threat (personal, social, and aesthetic) will be examined in order to discover their rhetorical strategies.

The personal threat is, at the same time, the most frightening and the most effective. It shows the greatest amount of irrationality on the part of an enemy who literally attacks the persona. An invasion of space often marks this aggression, since the satirist is attacked as a man, rather than as a poet. The first instance we see of this infringement on the persona's privacy occurs in Horace's Sermo 1.4 when Crispinus presents himself (14-16). Only one other invasion of privacy occurs for a Horatian persona, found in Sermo 1.10 (78-80). A minimal threat jeopardizes his privacy from one who would torment (*cruciet*) or taunt (*vellicet*) him.

The opening of Pope's "Epistle to Dr. Arbuthnot" provides the most sustained example of an intrusion, as the bad poets attempt to violate the sanctity of Twickenham and the fictive world of the poem itself. In the opening lines we are already aware that only a door separates the persona (and us) from this threat:

> P. SHUT, shut the door, good John! fatigued I said:
> Tie up the knocker, say I'm sick, I'm dead.
> The Dog-star rages! nay, 'tis past a doubt,
> All Bedlam, or Parnassus, is let out:
> Fire in each eye, and papers in each hand,
> They rave, recite, and madden round the land.
> (1-6)

The persona prefers to feign death rather than face the horde, which has previously been successful in invading his privacy. The following description is one of the most threatening in tone found in any literary satire:

> What walls can guard me, or what shades can hide?
> They pierce my thickets, thro' my Grot they glide,
> By land, by water, they renew the charge,
> They stop the chariot, and they board the Barge.
> No place is sacred, not the Church is free,

> Ev'n Sunday shines no Sabbath day to me:
> Then from the Mint walks forth the man of rhyme,
> Happy! to catch me just at Dinner time.
> (7-14)

In sharp contrast to such violence, the persona wishes only to be guarded by his walls, hidden by the shadows, or allowed to go peacefully to church and dinner. It is the ordinary routine and innocence conveyed by such wishes that increase the injustice of the excessive intrusions, made by suppliants who stop at no length to beg a favor of the great poet, and thereby stop his work. Such descriptions are developed in much greater detail in Pope than in Horace, forming vivid scenarios where the enemy is kept at a distance. But the door which John Searle clapped shut is on the verge of being broken down.

An invasion of privacy also occurs in Boileau's satires, especially in Satire IX. Paradoxically it is the persona who pursues himself, the persona's *je* corners his poetic *Esprit*. Yet an element of control restrains this invasion of privacy, since it is not the enemy himself who speaks but the poet who assumes the role of self-critic. The *je* functions like Pope's door to keep out the real enemies, allowing only a few of their muffled criticisms to enter into the closed security of the poetic discourse.

To some extent all threats represent a violation of the poet's right to privacy, but the examples cited above are most explicit. They not only constitute a Horatian topic adopted by the other poets, but are an effective means for the persona to gain immediate sympathy from the reader. The value of privacy need not be explained; the reader of the satires can readily perceive the injustice of the enemy's irrational and aggressive action. Subsequent charges the "useful enemy" makes are weakened by the reader's initial displeasure toward him, since the persona is cast in the role of an innocent victim.

The persona's privacy is threatened during his waking hours, and the restfulness of his sleep is also jeopardized. Horace's Sermo 2.1 describes the insomnia resulting when the satirist is unable to release his frustrations through verse (5-7). Pope relates a similar situation when his persona in "To Fortescue" is requested not to write satire:

> F. I'd write no more.
> P. Not write? but then I think,
> And for my soul I cannot sleep a wink:
> I nod in company, I wake at night,
> Fools rush into my head, and so I write.
> (11-15)

He combines the theme of intrusion with that of insomnia. When the reader learns that satire has a therapeutic value for the persona, he again is more sympathetic. Undisturbed sleep, like personal privacy, carries its own intrinsic value; when denied, the persona's satiric reaction appears justified.

The most serious, and most frequent, of the personal threats made against the satirist is death. The enemy threatens to stop the satirist permanently. Horace first mentions it in Sermo 2.1:

> seu me tranquilla senectus
> exspectat seu mors atris circumvolat alis, ...
> (57-58)

> whether peaceful age awaits me,
> or Death hovers round with sable wings, ...

The theme of the satirist's valiant stance against the background of possible death becomes a topic for Boileau and Pope, who translate freely the passage into their own works. Curiously enough, the "sable wings" of death remain a consistent image for all three, adding a tone of melodrama, as well as a metaphoric anonymity as to the precise source of the death threat. Boileau in Satire VII (63-72) echoes the Horatian passage, as does Pope in "To Fortescue" (92-104). The threat of death does not deter any from writing satire, even when possible assassins are named. Whether coming from friends or satiric victims, the fatal threats are clearly unjustified responses to the artistic expression which provoked them. Because they are aimed at him as a man, they are more comprehensible (than aesthetic reasons) to a greater number of readers. The persona is again portrayed as an innocent victim, as he persuades the reader to accept his side of the dispute.

Another group of threats can be categorized as social or societal in nature. They endanger the satirist's position in society, as the enemy argues that satire is either illegal or unsocial. The most serious of these threats is the charge of its illegality, which would surely stop the satirist if it could be proved true.[2] Both Horace (Sermo 2.1, 80-83) and Pope describe such a possible legal injunction:

> F. Your plea is good; but still I say, beware!
> Laws are explained by men -- so have a care.
> It stands on record, that in Richard's times
> A man was hanged for very honest rhymes.
> Consult the statute, quart. I think it is,
> Edwardi sext. or prim. et quint. Eliz.
> See Libels, Satires -- here you have it -- read.
> ("Fortescue," 143-49)

The legal threat must be answered carefully, since it does not seem unjustified nor does it create sympathy for the persona. Instead, it represents a very real obstacle; but once it is overcome, the persona is assured of future triumph.

He is also threatened with a loss of friends and readers because of his satires. The *amicus* might betray the satirist (Sermo 2.1, 60-62). Both Boileau and Pope describe situations in which the persona is cautioned against possible social disapproval (Satire IX, 117-22; "Epilogue to the Satires, Dialogue I," 23-26). The threat is significant for all three poets who believed not only in the social utility of satire, but also in the great value of friendship. The implicit charge that underlies these passages is that the persona cannot be both a satirist and a friend. It is intended to stop him from writing satire.

Related to the rupture in amical bonds is the possible loss of readers. Horace's persona states in _Sermo_ 1.4 that his satiric poems are unpopular. A satirist is to be avoided because he betrays friends for a laugh, and recites his verse inappropriately to any who will listen. Most readers are fearful of becoming too friendly with such a treacherous poet. A similar sentiment is also found in Boileau's _Satire_ VII (13-20). Fear and hatred for the satirist appear in Horace and Boileau as an attitude blocking communication and separating the poet from his readers. The question of the illegality and unsociability of his art poses a threat which must be answered. Whereas the personal threats really require no response, the social threats seriously jeopardize the success of each poem and the future of each satirist.

The aesthetic threats appear the most appropriate, since the enemy is using literary arguments to urge the satirist to stop writing satire. One of the most frequent is the command to write panegyric instead of satire. The interlocutor often urges the persona to redirect his energies in order to gain acceptance.[3] In Horace, the persona of _Sermo_ 2.1 is told to talk about Caesar (10-12). In this way the poet could continue to write, and he would be assured of many rewards. Boileau decides to try heroic verse in _Satire_ VII (21-24), and he receives the following suggestion in _Satire_ IX:

> Sans perdre en vains discours tout le fruit de vos
> veilles,
> Osez chanter du roi les augustes merveilles.
> Là, mettant à profit vos caprices divers,
> Vous verriez tous les ans fructifier vos vers;
> Et par l'espoir du gain votre Muse animée.
> Vendrait au poids de l'or une once de fumée.
> (31-36)

> Without losing in idle chatter the fruit of your
> effort,
> Try to sing about the grave marvels of the king.
> Thus, profiting from your various frivolities,

You will see your verse bear fruit each year.
And your Muse, driven by the hope of gain,
Will sell a little trifle as if it were gold.

Both passages expand the scope of the Horatian topic, while retaining the basic reason for a change in poetic genres: the "espoir du gain." Finally, similar advice is found in Pope's "To Fortescue" (21-22). Given the task of praising the "Caesar" of Augustan England, the persona is tempted by a title or the laureateship. Unlike the other threats we have examined, the command to try an alternative genre does not present an overt menace to the persona, but promises great rewards: personal security, friendship, and artistic recognition. All that is required in exchange is that the persona give up writing satire; which has been the intent of the satirist's enemy all along.

Another frequent literary threat facing all three poets is the suggestion to stop writing poetry altogether. This is the most extreme threat in this category, usually stated in a simple, unadorned style to maximize its effect. Trebatius suggests quite casually near the beginning of Sermo 2.1 that the persona should take a rest, and Fortescue simply advises "I'd write no more" (11). This is the essence of all the other kinds of threats, stated in the most basic, unequivocal terms. The persona in Boileau also faces it, but the context is more playful, with no direct proscription from another person. In Satire VII, having decided to "[quitter] la satire," the persona learns that panegyric only leads to frustration and poetic silence. And in Satire IX, the poet *je* suggests to his *Esprit* that silence is the best solution. Both in the playful context of Boileau and in the more serious tones of Horace and Pope, the threat of poetic silence is expressed as the suggestion of a "friendly" *adversarius*. Nonetheless, it is one of the most serious threats facing the persona, not only as a satirist, but more basically as a poet.

The alternatives to satire suggested to the persona (panegyric and silence) are the most frequent of the direct, literary threats to his continued career as a satirist. Other threats and charges are based on the poetry itself. The persona in Sermo 2.1 is accused of being too savage by some critics, too mild by others (1-3). A similar contradiction among critics is found in the opening to Pope's "To Fortescue:"

> P. THERE are (I scarce can think it, but am told)
> There are, to whom my satire seems too bold:
> Scarce to wise Peter complaisant enough
> And something said of Chartres much too rough.
> The lines are weak, another's pleased to say
> Lord Fanny spins a thousand such a day.
> (1-6)

This is an ingenious way to present criticisms of the persona's satire; it requires no response since the logical inconsistency cancels the two conflicting critical opinions. It is the same strategy which Pope expresses as a fervent plea in "Arbuthnot:" "May Dunce by dunce be whistled off my hands!" (254) With the contradictory criticism negating itself, the persona emerges as neither too savage nor too mild, in other words as a good, moderate satirist.

Among other complaints focused directly on the merit of the persona's poetry, the most surprising is the charge of plagiarism. Although Horace is never accused of it, Boileau and Pope are criticized for being too "Horatian". Both poets freely acknowledge their debt to Horace, yet their enemies try to silence them by claiming that their poetry is a mere translation. As with many of the threats, the accusation of plagiarism is an attempt to reduce the persona's poetic stature so that he appears mean, trifling, and unimportant.

Having been subjected to a barrage of abuse, the persona is faced with two possibilities: he can concede, or else respond with a self-defense. Although concession is not a real possibility, both Boileau and Pope use it in a playful, ironic context. It is not a Horatian topic; the personae in the Sermones never consider yielding, not even in jest. Yet Boileau claims a concession in each of his poems, with the greatest elaboration made in Satire IX:

> Toutefois, s'il le faut, je veux bien m'en dédire:
> Et pour calmer enfin tous ces flots d'ennemis,
> Réparer en mes vers les maux que j'ai commis.
> Puisque vous le voulez, je vais changer de style.
> Je le déclare donc: Quinaut est un Virgile.
> Pradon comme un Soleil en nos ans a paru.
> (284-89)

> Nonetheless, if need be, I am willing to retract:
> And, to calm this flood of enemies,
> Make amends in my verse for the harm I've done.
> Since you wish, I'll change my style.
> Therefore, I state: Quinault is a Virgil.
> Pradon brightens our days like the sun.

But the persona cannot concede in this way, because he is accused (and rightly so) of still mocking his enemies. Boileau's persona is forced to make a response and defend himself. Pope's persona also cannot quit, or yield to his critics. The power of vice is strong, tempting the persona in the first dialogue of the "Epilogue to the Satires" to forsake satire, "Adieu distinction, satire, warmth, and truth!" (64) But, when confronted with the scope and malignity of vice, the persona decides he must continue writing satire, no matter how ineffectual it may be.

In the second major division in the basic morphology, it is the persona's turn to present his arguments for continuing to write satire. This self-defense is often the longest section of each poem. The variety of responses, however, is more restricted than the variety of threats, and all responses proceed from a basic one: the persona claims to write a moral kind of satire. The main strategy is to deflect his enemies' threats and charges, which do not apply to his particular kind of satire.

The persona patiently endures the numerous invasions of his privacy. The specific threats of insomnia and death are not countered with any argumentation; they are simply rejected as deterrents to the satirist. Long responses are made, however, to the charges that satire is illegal or unsocial. It is here that the real argumentation of the persona begins. In response to the claim that his satire is illegal, two responses emerge. In Horace's Sermo 2.1, the pun on *mala* (malicious; poorly written) *carmina* (song) shows that the law does not apply to his satires, followed by a more substantive argument of political influence (Maecenas) assuring a favorable verdict. Similarly Pope claims that the law against satires does not apply to his "grave Epistles" protected by Walpole:

> P. Libels and Satires! lawless things indeed!
> But grave epistles, bringing vice to light ...
> Such as a king might read, a bishop write;
> Such as Sir Robert would approve ---.
> ("Fortescue," 150-53)

The case for the persona is clear and strong, with a humorous aesthetic reason followed quickly by a show of political power.

The persona's friendly alliance with a Maecenas or a Walpole is indicative of the value he places upon friendship and social bonds. While the basic response is an aesthetic claim for the morality of his satire, each satirist stresses the logical corollary that he himself is morally and socially responsible. Friendship is extremely important to these "civil" satirists, for whom the charge:

> Mais c'est un jeune fou qui se croit tout permis
> Et qui pour un bon mot va perdre vingt amis.
> (Sat. IX, 121-22)
>
> But he's a young fool, who takes liberties
> And who would lose twenty friends for a jest.

is simply not true. For both Horace and Boileau, friends are important as the audience, and not the victims, of their satires.

Pope makes the most references to friendship. In the second dialogue of the "Epilogue," the persona describes his honest friends who not only urge him to write poetry, but who approve of it:

> Yet think not, Friendship only prompts my lays; --
> I follow Virtue; where she shines, I praise: ...
> To find an honest man I beat about,
> And love him, court him, praise him, in or out.
> (94-95; 102-03)

Pope's persona would not sacrifice his friends for a satiric jest. Arbuthnot receives ample praise. At Twickenham or elsewhere, Pope's persona is surrounded with friends who support his satiric poetry. The charge of unsociability is not accurate, since he portrays himself as a very social and moral satirist.

As the topic of friendship suggests, each poet maintains a high ethical standard for himself in order to develop a sympathetic and credible ethos. The second half of *Sermo* 1.4 is devoted to a vivid description of the moral education of the persona. *Satire* VII shows the persona's moral discernment and high ethical expectations (55-56). And Pope's persona in "To Fortescue" is "Tim'rous by nature, of the rich in awe" (7). The portrayal of the persona as simple, honest, and ethically motivated is an important response to allegations of base raillery and immoral attack.[4]

The persona carefully builds his argument for his own civil morality, while seeking to preserve a modest self-image. He distinguishes himself from the real "poets" of the loftier genres. Each poet also makes a clear distinction between the kind of satire he is accused of writing and his own actual work. The satirist claims the same right, as all other readers have, to speak out freely and censure a bad piece of literature.[5] He also asserts that his style is open and honest, contrasted with the insinuating hypocrisy of slander.

The persona also describes essential characteristics of his work. He often explains what satire is not, and then what it is. Consistent with the portrayal of the satirist's ethical nature and the distinction between harsh calumny and honest satire, the satires themselves are described as ethically moral and unassumingly modest.[6] By defining the nature of his satire, the persona can answer the charges against him in such a way that he will be able to resolve the polemic in his favor and continue to write satire. The persona in Sermo 1.4 claims that his satire merely laughs at ineptitude, without biting maliciously (91-93). He promises that vice (*vitium*) and malice will never be found in his verse. The persona of Satire IX characterizes his activity as "je glose" (149) with a Muse who is "charitable et discrète" (211). And Pope is quite deferential in describing his "modest satire" (189) in "Arbuthnot".

The morality of their modest verse upholds a high principle: Virtue. Pope writes most frequently of the high principles which his satire serves. The persona of "Arbuthnot" explains that he:

> ...stoop'd [aimed] to Truth and moraliz'd his song:
> That not for Fame, but Virtue's better end,
> He stood the furious foe, the timid friend ....
> (341-43)

In closing the second dialogue of the "Epilogue" he claims the protection of Truth for his verse:

> Truth guards the poet, sanctifies the line.
> And makes immortal verse as mean as mine.
> (246-47)

The primary response of all three poets to their critics is contained in this exposition of the high moral mission of their poetry and its dedication to the principles of Virtue and Truth.[7]

In upholding Virtue the satirist is not alone, but sees himself as part of a long tradition of ethically moral and aesthetically superior satirists. Not only does the mention of this tradition answer the earlier charge of plagiarism, but it strengthens the satirist's main argument with examples of morally acceptable and critically approved predecessors. Although Horace is most frequently cited by later poets, beginning the lineage of moral satirists, he saw himself as part of an earlier tradition. In both Sermo 1.10 and 2.1, he defers to the reputation and stature of Lucilius. And preceding Lucilius in this lineage are the masters of Old Comedy. Boileau makes the most lengthy description of a tradition while arguing for the morality of satire and the safety of a satirist's career. In Satire IX the mention of predecessors serves another function; besides justifying himself by an association with the masters of satire, the persona satirizes his own critics:

> C'est ainsi que Lucile appuyé de Lélie,
> Fit justice en son temps des Cotins d'Italie,
> Et qu'Horace jetant le sel à pleines mains,
> Se jouait aux dépens des Pelletiers Romains.
> (275-78)

> It is thus that Lucilius, supported by Laelius,
> Meted out justice back then to the Cotins of Italy,
> And Horace, spinning witty comments,
> Enjoyed himself at the expense of the Roman
> Pelletiers.

Pope rarely discusses predecessors, and when he does he describes only the most recent poets in the tradition:

> Could pensioned Boileau lash, in honest strain,
> Flatterers and bigots, even in Louis' reign?
> Could laureate Dryden pimp and friar engage,
> Yet neither Charles nor James be in a rage?
> ("Fortescue," 111-14)

Examples of previous satirists, acceptable to public opinion and literary criticism, respond to earlier charges of immorality raised against the persona, as well as forecast his future success. For despite adverse criticism, none of the previous satirists quit writing satire. Neither will the persona.

The third and final morphological section concerns the triumph of the persona; the most concise and yet most important section. It briefly presents the result of the debate, coming as a logical addendum to the persona's response. Because of its position in the argument, the single statement of triumph is found near the end of each satire, providing both a resolution for the rhetorical argument and a climax for the fictive situation. It is the end point toward which the entire satire has been moving: the persona will continue to write satire.

In comparing the different satiric texts, we can see that the movement in them is reductive. Beginning with a multiplicity of threats, there is a more limited range of responses available to the persona, and the final triumph is described with the least amount of variation. Consequently, the one basic statement underlying the morphological section of triumph is much easier to apprehend, being more consistently and overtly expressed.

Minor triumphs occasionally occur in the course of the satire, providing a smaller climax to the narrative interest and clearing obstacles in the argumentation, allowing for the major, final triumph. For instance, the persona in "Arbuthnot" finally succeeds in establishing his privacy by shutting out the intruders. As for the social threats, all three poets register a triumph in their satires by describing their circle of friends and the group of poets who have accepted them. In terms of the legality of their verse, both _Sermo_ 2.1 and "To Fortescue" describe the final liberty of the persona from prosecution. Such minor triumphs resolve the personal and social threats to the persona, while the one major triumph in each satire resolves the basic aesthetic threat to his continued practice of satire.

In Sermo 2.1, the vow to continue writing satire is direct and explicit:

> dives, inops, Romae, seu fors ita iusserit, exsul,
> quisquis erit vitae scribam color.
> (59-60)

> Rich or poor, in Rome, or if chance so bid, in
> exile,
> Whatever the state of my life, I will write.

The future tense of *scribam* (I will write) makes it particularly powerful as a triumphant statement of continuation. In Boileau's satires the persona's triumph focuses on his will to continue. And for Pope, not only will he continue to write, but he will publish. The addition to the Horatian *scribam* is slight, but it reveals the insistence to communicate a satiric message. In the final, triumphant passage of "Arbuthnot," the persona seeks poetic liberty, and also general freedom to live as he chooses. It transcends the constraints on the persona's satire to encompass finally his entire life:

> O grant me, thus to live, and thus to die!
> Who spring from Kings shall know less joy than I...
> Me, let the tender office long engage,
> To rock the cradle of reposing Age,
> With lenient arts extend a Mother's breath,
> Make Langour smile, and smooth the bed of Death,
> Explore the thought, explain the asking eye,
> And keep a while one parent from the sky! ...
> A. Whether that blessing be deny'd or giv'n,
> Thus far was right, the rest belongs to Heav'n.
> (404-05, 08-13, 18-19)

The satire ends with an appeal to divine providence in the most comprehensive triumph.

The detailed examination of the three morphological sections of threat, response, and triumph has revealed one basic plot pattern underlying all the satires in our study. Although vast differences among them appear on a surface level, they have basic similarities. In all poems an initial threat for the persona to stop writing satire is met by his response, explaining the morality and correctness of *his* kind of satire, and prompting a final statement of triumph and continuation. He seeks freedom from attack and vows to keep writing satire.

Most of the structuring devices and strategies in literary satire have a basis in the Horatian *Sermones*, retained by Boileau and Pope as traditional structures and also as rhetorically effective methods for persuading the reader. Persuasive effectiveness is the greatest strength of the plot structure. Finally, the form of the plot is necessitated by the role of the persona. In order to understand how the persona shapes the plot in literary satire, and why a plot is absent in the *Arts of Poetry*, we will next examine the characterization of the persona in the two different forms of poetry.

CHAPTER V

THE CONTRAST OF FORMS

Si paulum summo decessit, vergit ad imum.
(_Ars_, 378)

If it falls from the top in the least, it
sinks to the bottom.

In theory, only two levels of poetry exist for our satirist-critics, the very best (*summo*) and the worst (*imum*). Anything less than excellent falls to the bottom of Parnassus as a failure. The hierarchy of good and bad poets is simplified, with an immense void between the poles of excellence and failure. One exception stands out: each poet places his satiric persona in a medial position between the extremes, half way up Parnassus.

We have already seen that the personae display a great deal of modesty in responding to their enemies' charges. Such modesty is rhetorically necessary. If the personae were to claim that their own verse were excellent, they would not be as credible or persuasive -- they would be open themselves to further attack from new enemies exposing imperfections. Their self-aggrandizement could be ridiculed, and their folly denounced. The personae suggest they are good, but not great; and their triumph consists of a continuation of their past efforts, not in proving the excellence of their work.

The standard of excellence in poetry is represented by a few poets elevated above the persona. Yet many poets are far below him. In _Sermo_ 1.4 Horace's persona is not on the same level with Eupolis, Cratinus, Aristophanes, or Ennius. But he is a better poet than the windbag Crispinus or the libelers Sulcius and Caprius. In both Sermo 1.10 and 2.1, he is beneath Lucilius, but he lives among the great. This reveals an ambiguous mixture of modesty and grandeur, characteristic of a secondary position. He allows himself a modest success by association.

The personae in Boileau's literary satires are also placed in a medial position between the extremes of good and bad poets. In Satire VII, the persona repeats the Horatian distinction between poets and versifiers as he modestly describes his own poetic abilities. He has no poetic reputation yet, but this is preferable to the infamy of the "perfect fools" and the "cold rhymesters" whom he encounters in quantity. Superior to such poetasters, the persona is nonetheless below the rank of Horace and Juvenal. In Satire II, the persona defers to the poetic mastery of Molière (whether sincerely or ironically). Yet hard work elevates his poetry over the careless verse of Scudéry:

> Bienheureux Scudéry, dont la fertile plume
> Peut tous les mois sans peine enfanter un volume!
> (77-78)
>
> Lucky Scudéry, whose fertile pen
> Can effortlessly hatch a volume every month!

Painfully aware of his own imperfections, the persona constantly strives to achieve excellence.

In Satire IX, the *je* pushes his *Esprit* further down Mount Parnassus, but the *Esprit* claims to be inspired as he advances upward. The tension of the two actions places the persona in a secondary position, dynamically verging on the summit of excellence. Although none of the personae in Boileau's literary satires pretends to rival Horace, Juvenal or Molière, they are much further up the mountain than Pelletier, Scudéry, or Chapelain. Examples of poets at both extremes serve to situate clearly the persona and his poetic ability in each of the satires.

Both good and bad poets are mentioned in Pope's satires, but the persona's medial position between them is not as clear as with Boileau, since the hierarchy is not as concisely stated. But the persona in Pope does occupy a medial position. In the "Epistle to Dr. Arbuthnot" he is compared to the Classical masters, but his imperfections are described in physical (not poetic) terms:

> There are, who to my person pay their court:
> I cough like Horace, and though lean am short, ...
> All that disgraced my Betters, met in me. --
> Say for my comfort, languishing in bed,
> "Just so immortal _Maro_ held his head:"
> And when I die, be sure you let me know
> Great Homer died three thousand years ago.
> (115-16, 120-24)

Although he is considered imperfect, the context for judging the persona entails the Ancients. In addition, similar to the personae in the _Sermones_, he is accepted by the best poets of his age and benefits from a greatness by association (Congreve, Swift). Modestly assuming a position below the stature of such poets, the persona is far superior to hordes of scribblers (Burnet, Oldmixon). The bands of poor poets believe themselves that the persona is a better poet than they, since they seek his advice and friendship. Both friends and petitioners place him near the first rank of poets, although he modestly excludes himself from the select group of recognized masters.

The secondary position that the personae of Horace, Boileau, and Pope occupy in the literary satires seems to contradict their theoretical statement that no rank is possible between poetic greatness and failure. While the two extremes are static, with a permanence implied in Homer's supremacy or Scudéry's inferiority, the persona's position is a dynamic element in the static hierarchy. A poetic excellence is implied, but not overtly stated.

The secondary position of the persona also reveals that

his poetic career is still in process. It is not an accomplished fact that can be objectively judged. The very writing of the literary satire is part of an on-going process that may lead to excellence, but which has not yet arrived. In fact, the literary satires themselves ocupy a medial position in the satires of each poet, since none was either the first nor the last satire. In the middle of his career as a satirist, each defended his previous work by the dynamic plot of literary satire, in which he responded to critic-enemies by explaining the process of his particular kind of satire. And because of his medial position as a poet, the persona is forced to argue his self-defense at length.

In contrast, the poems of literary theory (<u>Arts of Poetry</u>) are not structured in the same way. The persona does not have the same role of a modestly medial poet, nor is there a plot which defends his previous poetry. Although the extremes of poetic value are discussed, the perspective is different, and the formal structure shifts from that of the literary satires. In the satires the focus is directed to the persona, who encloses himself in his own protective satire. The addressee is included in this self-contained discourse as a confidant, an intermediary between the persona and the world. But in the <u>Arts of Poetry</u>, the focus is shifted onto the addressee; the text is no longer "self"-centered, but directed toward another. The movement is linear, not circular. And the role of the persona and the addressee change significantly. We will examine the roles of the persona and addressee in the three theoretical poems, and the possibility of a plot.

The persona is not a modest poet, in fact, he is hardly a poet at all. The shift in his role from poet to advisor occurs within the <u>Ars poetica</u>, expressed in the following essential passage:

> ergo fungar vice cotis acutum
> reddere quae ferrum valet, exsors ipsa secandi;

munus et officium, nil scribens ipse, docebo,
unde parentur opes, quid alat formetque poetam,
quid deceat, quid non, quo virtus, quo ferat error.
(304-08)

So I'll play a whetstone's part
Which makes steel sharp, but of itself cannot cut;
Though I write nothing myself, I will teach the poet's office and duty,
From where he draws his stores, what nurtures and fashions him,
What benefits him and what not, where the right and wrong paths lead.

While not writing anything himself, he will act as a whetstone (*cos*) and teach others how to write. Earlier in the poem the persona had described his own career, rejecting the title of *poeta* and preferring to be called a *scriptor* (writer). But references like these to the persona as a poet disappear from the Ars poetica after the key passage in which he assumes the role of whetstone. Instances of his role as critic and teacher are more noticeable after the passage (317-18, 351-53, 408-11).

The persona no longer refers to himself and his own poetic practice, but he advises the Pisos. The focus is directed to the future excellence of their poetry, rather than to the defense of the persona's previous writing. In the Ars poetica, the Piso brothers are the main poets; the poem is addressed to them, with an intent to improve their poetry. Throughout the work they are addressed as writers, and their role does not change. The direction of the entire poem from the critic *ego* to the Pisones as poets can be seen in the numerous imperatives that instruct them on the details of the art of poetry. The imperative mood instructs, demands credibility, and focuses on the addressee rather than on the speaker. From the "credite" (believe me) of line 6 to the "tolle memor" (remember) of line 368, imperatives form a structural chain in the Ars poetica, as they convey precepts from the advising persona to the young poets.

In Boileau's Art poétique, similar roles are assumed by the persona and the addressee.[1] Only at the end of *Chant* IV, in the concluding lines of the poem, does the persona refer to himself as a poet (223-26). Even in this passage the persona is reticent about his poetic powers, especially in a genre other than satire. Within the poem itself his primary function is that of a reader-critic, an arbiter of *bon goût* (good taste). We first encounter him reading a pastoral novel (I, 57-58), and later we see him attending a play (III, 29-32). In both instances he takes the perspective of a member of the audience, explaining his reaction to a piece of literature.[2] The persona then advises his protégé, the addressee, on how to achieve excellence in poetry.

The addressee in the Art poétique is anonymous; he is the ideal young poet capable of the best. The opening passage, while dissuading false poets from a poetic career, implies the innate character of the idealized poet for whom the Art poétique is written:

> C'est en vain qu'au Parnasse un téméraire auteur
> Pense de l'art des vers atteindre la hauteur.
> (1-2)
>
> It is foolhardy for a bold author on Parnassus,
> To think he can reach the top of the art of poetry.

The addressee is not a "bold author," and in order for him to achieve the height of poetry, it is assumed that he has a natural genius that distinguishes a true poet. The theory contained in an Art of Poetry needs to be coupled with natural talent. A true poet must burn with fires of enthusiasm, persevere on the difficult path to perfection, and possess a *bel Esprit* (good mind). In the text, he is idealized, a representative type, and not a real poet; he exists primarily to be formed into a great poet by the persona. That is the reason for the lack of information about who he is, whereas the entire poem explains what he will be if he follows the persona's numerous imperatives. Because he possesses the poetic potential of all beginning poets, the addressee is a collective mask for a variety of possible poets. It appears that the same *vous* is addressed in discussing each genre, even though:

La nature, fertile en esprits excellents,
Sait entre les auteurs partager les talents.
(I, 13-14)

Nature, fertile in excellent minds,
Is able to divide talents among the authors.

But the addressee in the Art poétique is a generalized character who represents all poetic talent, every young poet worthy to begin a career of writing. The persona directs his advisory imperatives to this fictional ideal, relating his wisdom as a critic and reader to the next generation of writers. The imperatives that transfer this wisdom are more numerous than in the Ars poetica or the Essay on Criticism, and they are noticeable for their frequency and colloquial tone: "N'allez pas" (Don't go), "Fuyez" (Flee), "Soyez" (Be), and "Aimez" (Espouse).[3] With such imperatives the persona is a guide rather than a poet.[4] He has no need to defend his past poetry, and his opinions on poetry are credibly stated in his simple, natural, authoratative commands.

In the Essay on Criticism, Pope's persona is virtually absent. Throughout the poem he acts as an advisor, but seldom refers to himself. The self-descriptions reveal the persona in his other role, as a poet (419). As with Boileau, the most complete statement of the persona as poet occurs at the end of the poem, although in the Essay the allusion is veiled by Pope's reference to himself as "Muse"[5]:

Such late was Walsh -- the Muse's judge and friend,
Who justly knew to blame or to commend ...
(Her guide now lost) no more attempts to rise,
But in low numbers short excursions tries ....
(729-30, 737-38)

Avoiding a direct portrayal of his persona, Pope expresses himself both in the customary imperatives of the other Arts *of Poetry*, and in numerous first-person plural references ("we"). He generalizes himself, his reader, and all people of taste in a community of critics for whom he is the spokesman. It is primarily through the voice of the generalized "we", and the numerous imperatives, that the addressee is advised. In this way, Pope assumes two roles in the *Essay*: the primary role of the advisor-critic within the "we", and the poet "I". Yet neither Pope nor his previous poetry is the focus of the *Essay*.

The primary emphasis is placed upon the addressee and his future role as a critic; all the advice, rules, and dogma are directed at him so that he may achieve the fame of an excellent critic. The ideal critic both gives and receives fame, upholding the nobility of his art of criticism. Like the persona, he also will guide young poets and critics with his superior judgment. In order to achieve this goal, the imperatives and guidelines of the *Essay* direct the addressee to a proper understanding of poetry and criticism. The "you", future critic and poet, is an abstract construct, a paragon of literary excellence, capable of reaching the summit of Mount Parnassus.

In all three theoretical poems the role of the persona (and addressee) has differed significantly from that of the literary satires. The persona is no longer a poet, but he functions primarily as an advisor to the addressee. Emphasis is not placed on the past satires of the persona, but on the future potential of the addressee. The modesty and self-defense of the literary satires is gone, and the medial position of the persona is replaced by the primary position of the idealized addressee on the height of Parnassus. Differences between the two forms of literature are exemplified in the characters, and also in the plot.

In the literary satires, the threat, response, and triumph constitute the three stages of the plot. The persona occupies a central position, and his response which justifies his previous satires is the most developed section. The movement in the _Arts of Poetry_ shows that the audience and its reaction to poetry occupies a greater place, and the persona portrays himself as a reader advising the future poet, the addressee. The threat is no longer directed at the persona, but at an audience bored with bad poetry. Neither the persona nor the addressee is threatened; the former withdraws as a poet, and the latter has not yet begun to write. The response section, in which the persona advises the addressee with the rules and dogma of good poetry, is also the most developed section, but it merges with the addressee's triumph, since his future poetry will follow the advice exactly. The hypothetical nature of the addressee presupposes that the rules will be fully realized. And because the response and triumph sections are the same, a two stage progression occurs in the _Arts of Poetry_, characterized by an alternation between the faults of bad poetry and rules for good poetry. There is no medial position, nor a three stage plot, but only the best and the worst in literature.

The alternation between the two extremes provides a structure to the _Arts of Poetry_, although it is not as complex nor as dynamic as that in the literary satires. The series of alternations are not clearly or structurally unified. The theoretical poems are also quite long, and often lack transitions in thought; the main structure seems to be a compilation, rather than an organized plot. But thematic and structural patterns do organize parts of the poem.[6]

In Horace's poem we can observe the usual order of the two extremes: a fault is described, followed by advice on means to avoid it. The introductory lines present a ridiculous, disorganized picture:

> Humano capiti cervicem pictor equinam
> iungere si velit, et varias inducere plumas ...
> (1-2)

> If a painter chose to join a human head to the neck of a horse,
> And to spread feathers of different colors ...

while the rest of the poem describes rules to achieve order and a proper balance of parts. In the Ars poetica, neither the fault nor the advice is described at length. The process of exposition and analysis involved in a plot is not present, but we are given only a quick succession of opposing views.

A similar pattern exists in many sections of the Art poétique. In discussing poetic invention, the mania for novelty is contrasted with advice to avoid its excess:

> La plupart emportés d'une fougue insensée
> Toujours loin du droit sens vont chercher leur pensée.
> Ils croiraient s'abaisser, dans leurs vers monstrueux,
> S'ils pensaient ce qu'un autre a pu penser comme eux.
>
> (I, 39-42)
>
> Evitons ces excès. Laissons à l'Italie,
> De tous ces faux brillants, l'éclatante folie.
> Tout doit tendre au Bon sens ....
>
> (I, 43-45)
>
> Most are carried away in a senseless flight
> They seek their ideas far from the right road.
> They would feel humiliated, in their monstruous verse,
> If they thought that another could think like they.
>
> Avoid these excesses. Leave to Italy
> The brilliant folly of all these garish adornments.
> Everything must lead toward good sense ....

The most prominent use of the pattern of opposition occurs in *Chants* II and III, with the proposal for generic distinctions. The common faults which bad poets make are first mentioned, often in humorous descriptions. The addressee is advised on the means to best succeed in each genre. In Boileau's poem, the alternations betwen bad and good poetry help move the reader through the text, by means of contrasting examples which both teach and delight.

The series of oppositions in all three theoretical poems does not create a uniform or sustained plot, but rather a shift propelling the reader from the extreme of bad poetry to advice for the best. He is persuaded to accept the advice, since the authority of the persona is credible, and the advice is a rational means to avoid serious fault. The recurrent topics in the _Arts of Poetry_ are less personal than those of the satires, focused instead on theory. The threat to the reader, from disorder, pride, dullness, and nonsense, replace the threats to the persona from trials, death, insomnia, and the invasion of privacy. Yet some of the topics from one form occur in the other. In the literary satires, invasion of the persona's privacy is a common theme, found also in _Arts of Poetry_:

> No place so sacred from such fops is barred,
> Nor is Paul's church more safe than Paul's church-yard;
> Nay, fly to altars; there they'll talk you dead;
> For fools rush in where angels fear to tread.
> (_Essay_, 622-25)

Conversely, many topics of the _Arts of Poetry_ appear in the literary satires; the faults of poetic disorder and irrational poets underlying the theoretical poems are also criticized in the literary satires:

> Tes [Scudéry] écrits, il est vrai, sans art, et languissants,
> Semblent être formés en dépit du bon sens ....
> (_Sat_. II, 79-80)

> Your writings, it is true, artless and languishing,
> Seem to be formed in spite of good sense ....

Despite the structural differences which separate the two forms of literature, and lead to dissimilar rhetorical goals, a similarity of content exists between them. Basic correspondences unite them, since both forms evaluate poetic practices in a hierarchy of *laus et vituperatio* (praise and blame). They are closely related both in content and tone, sharing satiric and theoretical passages. Their structures, however, emphasize different aspects of the content and shape it so that the reader is moved in separate directions.

CHAPTER VI

THE INTERPHASE OF TONES

We have attempted, up to this point, to keep literary satire separate from literary theory, but we will now see the extent to which they are interrelated. A unity of content underlies them. Both forms discuss the same topic, and concentrate on converse values at the opposite extremes of poetic evaluation. In addition, satires can be theoretical and theory can be satiric.

In general, less theory appears in satire than satiric passages in the Arts of Poetry. The genre satire is a shorter form, allowing less scope for the development of theoretical statements, which need room to develop, clarify themselves, and provide their own context. In contrast, the satiric tone purposefully disrupts the theoretical flow, and may be achieved more quickly by a single word or expression.

The poetry of Horace exemplifies the unity of the two forms. In Sermo 1.4, relatively few theoretical passages state in direct terms the requirements for good poetry. In the opening of the poem, Eupolis, Cratinus and Aristophanes are given the title *poetae*, but the only reasons given for this honor are their social utility and their frankness of expression. The most complete statement on literary theory occurs as the persona excludes himself from the body of *poetae*:

> ingenium cui sit, cui mens divinior atque os
> magna sonaturum, des nominis huius honorem.
> (43-44)

If one has gifts inborn, a soul divine, and tongue
Of noble utterance, to such give the honor of that
name.

To write with a metrically patterned line or in a chatty, prosaic style does not qualify as "writing properly." The correct poet is possessed of the gift of *ingenium* (genius), a *mens divinior* (more divine mind), and an *os magna sonaturum* (mouth about to speak great things). The actual craft of poetry is not mentioned. In any event, the ideal poet is possessed of tho same qualities that are later ascribed to Greeks in the Ars poetica, providing a theoretical link between the two works: "Grais ingenium, Grais dedit ore rotundo / Musa loqui" (To the Greeks the Muse gave genius, and speech in well rounded phrase, 323-24). After having described the poet, Sermo 1.4 discusses the deficiency of comedy. It needs to have "spiritus ac vis" (life and force, 46); these qualities reside in the work, not in its manner of recitation. Similarly, in the Ars poetica, drama is required to touch and move the spectator rather than indulge in theatrical bluster (95-100). Its intrinsic force must even survive rearrangement of its parts (more possible in Latin). A proper accord between words and content, moving the spectator, is the hallmark of excellent poetry. The most important contributions of Sermo 1.4, then, are the description of the good poet and the distinction between poetry and versification.

Sermo 1.10, an *apologia* (defense) of earlier statements about Lucilius, contains key critical terms. The persona criticizes the verse of Lucilius as *incomposito* (irregular), implying a standard of technical excellence and order, while at the same time praising Lucilius' use of *sal* (salt) to rub down the city. Freedom of expression is extolled, while technique (especialy of metrics) is the center of attention and cause for criticism. The main theoretical passage in Sermo 1.10 proposes brevity, variety, and restraint as essential elements of good poetry (7-17). The goal of laughter is not sufficient, since a satire must also be well written. Its effect is even greater if well expressed, and the thought runs (*currat*, 9) to an immediate effect. Brevity concerns not only style and content, but the rhetorical effect of the entire poem.

The poet is also required to vary his style. In the case of the satirist, the extremes of the sad (*modo tristi*) and the happy (*iocoso*) are available, with an occasional use of wit. Although this is good advice, the method of its application is left to the poet's discretion. And the poet must restrain his force and wit, suggested also in the Ars poetica (265, 292-94). Wit, a controlled form of violence, is restrained further by the poetic demands of "correct" satire, which makes it even more effective.

In discussing the selection of satire as his genre, with the underlying theoretical supposition that a poet can excel in only one genre, the persona describes the current literary situation. Genres are described, and poets named. One basic concern which underlies all such diverse work is the need for revision:

> saepe stilum vertas, iterum quae digna legi sint
> scripturus, neque te ut miretur turba labores,
> contentus paucis lectoribus.
> (72-74)

> Often must you turn your pencil to erase, if you
> hope to write something
> Worth a second reading, and you must not strive to
> catch the wonder of the crowd
> But be content with the few as your readers.

The adverb *saepe* (often) is one of the more significant words of the passage, indicating the exacting, time-consuming craft of the poet. The subjunctive verb exhorts the poet to work, in order to increase the merit (*digna*) of the poem. Although poorly written verse may please the crowd, the serious and dignified poet constantly revises his work for it to be worthy of the select few. The satire in Sermo 1.10 is directed at the *incompositus* verse of Lucilius, but the theoretical statements do not directly concern him nor satire as a genre. They are not as epigrammatic or memorable as those in Sermo 1.4, but considerable substance lies behind the *apologia* of Lucilius.

Sermo 2.1 is the most personal and anecdotal of the three. Rich in implications concordant with the general corpus of Horace's work, it contains few openly stated theories. Trebatius urges his friend to write panegyric, implying a hierarchical value of genres. The persona's insistence on his poetic liberty to write satire is noteworthy, but it is not explored at length. The pun on the *mala* (evil, poorly written) *carmina* (song) provides the most tangibly theoretical statement. According to the persona's playful argument, the greater evil is not satire itself, but poorly written verse, for which there is no legal redress. It is, ultimately, an overriding principle in Horatian theory: bad poetry is inexcusable. The theoretical statements in the Sermones and the Ars poetica provide a standard for testing *bona carmina.*

Because poorly written poetry is unacceptable, it is not criticized, but satirized. Satiric passages in the Ars poetica, marked by an emotionalism and excess beyond objective criticism, invoke scorn and ridicule rather than mere disapproval.[1] Ridicule and laughter are the audience's response to poetic failure, with reference to satiric laughter occurring in the introductory passage: "spectatum admissi risum teneatis, amici?" (Could you, my friends, if favored with a private view, refrain from laughing?, 5). Although the persona does not claim this response of satiric ridicule as a procedure used in the Ars poetica itself, it seems clear that derisive laughter is purposefully evoked in several passages.[2] Three of them are significant for their similarity of tone and theme, in which a mad, disordered artist is satirized.

The first, in the poem's introduction, is relatively mild in tone. The poem begins with a reference to the human form perverted by the disorganized fantasies of the painter. Such a picture evokes laughter, as would the empty (*vanae*, 7) thoughts of a sick man. Order and consistency are the standards, and deviations represent ridiculous fantasy. When Democritus, a mad poet first appears, the attack becomes more personal:

> ingenium misera quia fortunatius arte
> credit et excludit sanos Helicone poetas
> Democritus, bona pars non unguis ponere curat,
> non barbam, secreta petit loca, balnea vitat.
> (295-98)

> Because Democritus believes that native talent
> Is a greater boon than wretched art, and shuts out
> from Helicon sane poets,
> Many don't clip their nails or shave their beards,
> They haunt lonely places and shun the baths.

Ingenium (genius) is praised elsewhere in the Horatian texts, but when it is the poet's only source and method (without craftsmanship), then the persona would rather renounce poetry. Although the renunciation is playful and ironic, it still carries a literal meaning. The persona is the standard of judgment, whose critical "fingernail" (*unguem*, 294) contrasts with Democritus' appearance. The long nails and beard, unsociability and general filth of Democritus correspond to an unkempt kind of poetry. The attack is swift and complete. The Ars poetica concludes with a scornful look at the worst of all poets:

> vesanum tetigisse timent fugientque poetam
> qui sapiunt: agitant pueri incautique sequuntur.
> hic, dum sublimis versus ructatur et errat ....
> (455-57)

> Men of sense fear to touch a crazy poet, and run
> away,
> Children tease and pursue him rashly,
> He, head held high, sputters verse and strays off.

The outcast poet is like one with distemper, a frenetic lunatic. The standard of judgment are "those who know" (*qui sapiunt*), and even little children are not blamed for their teasing cruelty. Sputtering verses distractedly, the self-destructive poet is not despaired. Three times the theme of death appears, with the assumption that such a madman deserves it Failing to meet the standard of being a man, and suspected of blasphemy, he is finally compared to an animal: a bear howling his verse, or a leech draining his victims. Even an Ars poetica will not make him a civil, technically-refined poet.

Other targets of satire are mentioned in the poem besides mad poets. Extremes of poetic style are gently ridiculed. The images of swelling and creeping appear in a discussion of the drama (93-98). The excesses of bombast and pedestrian prose are to be avoided, or the audience will surely laugh. This discerning audience is an elite corps, for the masses are satirized (210, 224, 249-50). All the satiric victims, from the mad poets to the bean-buying spectators, are made to appear ridiculous (if not dangerous).

The theoretical statements in Boileau's literary satires are more personal in tone and more exclusively concerned with writing satire than was seen in the Horatian Sermones. Boileau's personae express theoretical statements describing the poet's own practice of writing satire, and satire as a genre. Satire VII states the persona's intentions in writing satire:

> Le mérite pourtant m'est toujours précieux:
> Mais tout fat me déplaît et me blesse les yeux.
> (55-56)
>
> Merit, however, has always been precious to me:
> But every fool displeases me, and hurts my eyes.

In this passage *grâce* is opposed to satire as the persona intends to spare the lash and grant charity toward some people. But once he has taken up his pen and come under the influence of his poetic verve, the writing of poetry necessitates judgment and choice. Satire VII also provides details on Roman satirists (73-79). The "witty words" of Horace characterize his urbane style, concealing bile and revenge. Virtue is considered the standard of excellence in this passage, whereas in the Art poétique Horace is pictured as defending "truth;" but both passages are similar in tone. In Satire VII Boileau lifts "the mask off vice;" in the Art poétique (II,148) he holds "A mirror up to vice." As for Juvenal, he uses a "biting pen" in the Satire, and a "biting hyperbole" in the Art poétique (II, 158) while rebuking his fellow Romans. The criticism of both Roman satirists maintains the theoretical stance that satire, whether urbane or mordant, upholds an ethical value.

In Satire II, the persona expresses great concern over the precision of vocabulary and the need to revise:

> Ainsi, recommençant un ouvrage vingt fois,
> Si j'écris quatre mots, j'en effacerai trois.
> (51-52)
>
> Thus, starting a work twenty times over,
> If I write four words, I erase three.

Care is needed in order to fulfill the Horatian injunction of writing properly (*poliment*, 72). Here the real work of poetry is described, work that presupposes an art of poetry. As in the Art poétique itself (and Horace), both genius and art are valued. It is not enough to please the crowds, but one must strive for perfection. The final theoretical statement on the sublime (91-96) is an important summary of Boileau's theory of poetry.

In Satire IX theoretical statements are also inserted into the satire. The necessary prerequisite of genius, an *esprit divin* (divine mind), is mentioned here, as in the introductory passage of the Art poétique. Similar in tone and content to the descriptions of satire in Satire VII and the Art poétique, the polarized ethical values of virtue and vice are discussed with the terms "error," "pride," and "vice" which are opposed to "reason." The influence of Horatian theory is readily apparent, with the *plaisant et utile* (pleasant and useful) function of satiric poetry expressing the *utile dulci* of Horace. In general, the theoretical statements in the Satires are marked by a singleness of purpose, to justify satire, with only small variations on the topic.

Satire is more frequent in the Art poétique than in Horace's or Pope's theoretical poems, and the greater frequency offers a variety of subject matter and technique. Nonetheless, general characteristics of the satiric tone emerge: it is sharp and direct, focused on individuals, and maintains a standard of both ethics and reason. The mad poet of the Ars poetica gives way to Boileau's fool (*sot*). Although the Art poétique is filled with rules, writers are not satirized specifically for breaking them. Only once in the approximately forty passages of satire is deviation from a rule, namely that of *vraisemblance*, the cause of satire (III, 39-42). The greatest fault for a poet is to fail the overall goal of poetry, to *plaire et toucher* (please and move). Cold, boring, imprecise poems arouse the satiric ire, and wit, of the persona.

The Art poétique does not contain a satiric frame like the Ars poetica, but within a serious frame satire abounds.[3] The persona acknowledges it as one of his techniques:

> Et pour finir par un trait de satire,
> Un sot trouve toujours un plus sot qui l'admire.
> (I, 231-32)
>
> And to finish with a satiric barb,
> A fool always finds one more foolish to admire him.

The targets are people, but they are types without a name.[4] Whereas the Satires are noted for their device of "naming names," only half of the satiric passages in the Art poétique use names. Many of the familiar names from the Satires

(1661-1668) are gone from the Art poétique (1674): Chapelain, Cotin, and the abbé de Pure. Scudéry is still satirized; Saint-Amant and Ronsard are new to be named as targets. But the more expanded use of general types enlarges the scope of the satire in the Art poétique.

Another noteworthy feature of the theoretical poem is the satiric scene, rich in metaphoric imagery. Saint-Amant is satirized in such a vignette, based on his Moïse sauvé. Satiric tableaux are found throughout the Art poétique, from the figurative description of the flourishing of burlesque (I, 85-88) to the lengthiest scene of all, portraying Claude Perrault (III, 1-24). They enliven the text and provide their own closed, metaphoric context in order to effect a rapid and picturesque condemnation. Caught up in the imagery of burlesque as a contagion, or Perrault as an incompetent doctor, the reader becomes an accomplice of the satirist as he accepts, and enjoys, the extended metaphor.

Ethical criteria figure prominently in the satiric passages concerning bad poets and bad poetry. Pride, folly, and excess characterize Boileau's bad poet:

> Mais souvent un esprit qui se flatte, et qui s'aime
> Méconnaît son génie, et s'ignore soi-même.
> (I, 19-20)
>
> But often a mind which flatters and adores itself
> Misjudges its strengths, and is self-ignorant.

Self ignorance for a poet is fatal to his art, obscuring his powers and production. He must know himself in order to write well, and evidences of pride furnish much satiric material. The charge of folly is a more general fault, indicating a widespread deviation from reason. It is a common complaint, judging by the frequency of the ever-present monosyllables *sot* and *fat*. But if the good poet and reader flee from bad poetry, what is its ultimate fate?

Several locales are cited as graveyards, creating a special kind of satire describing the appropriate uses of doggerel verse. One place mentioned is Pont neuf, with its carnival atmosphere (I, 97; III, 427-28). And, if the poems are bad, at least the paper may be useful for wrapping up merchandise:

> Le reste aussi peu lu que ceux de Pelletier,
> N'a fait de chez Sercy qu'un saut chez l'épicier.
> (II, 100-01)
>
> The rest, as little read as those [works] of Pelletier,
> Took a quick jump from the bookstall to the market.

The worst fate of all is oblivion in the bookstore (III, 331-32; IV, 47-48). This is the fate of all poetry which does not measure up to the standard of the Art poétique. The proud and ignorant poet, cold and weak verse, all provide material for satire in the poem; but it is the image of the unsold, deteriorating book of poems that represents the most sobering picture of failure.

The entire process of bad writing, from inflated intentions to final decay, is described in the Art poétique. The satire of Boileau's persona is characterized by greater frequency and greater ethical content than was seen in Horace's Ars poetica. More names are used, but there are also many generalized types. In addition, the tone is sharper and more direct than in the Latin model. Finally, the general intent of Boileau's satire is to condemn poetry that is cold and boring, which fails to meet the primary standard: *plaire et toucher*.

Pope's Imitations of Horace contain theory which is more ethically oriented than the Sermones, and more generally applicable (not limited mainly to satire) than Boileau's Satires. Much of the ethical content consists of practical advice and commonplaces rather than a rigorous analysis of moral issues. Although most of the statements are provoked by the surrounding satiric context, presenting no discernible pattern or intent, a few main ideas recur. The poet's knowledge of himself and his own capabilities is not to be obscured by pride, flattery, or jealousy. Also, the virtues of the craftsman are stressed: restraint, dignity, and a persistence to revise. Although these themes were available to Pope from both Horace and Boileau, his treatment of them is nonetheless unique and inventive.

In the "Epistle to Dr. Arbuthnot," the theoretical passages vary greatly in content. The persona uses himself as an example, offering advice based on his own practical experience. His self-restraint and disregard for petty criticism are offered as a model for behavior:

> If want provoked, or madness made them print,
> I waged no war with Bedlam or the Mint.
> Did some more sober Critic come abroad;
> If wrong, I smiled; if right, I kissed the rod.
> (155-58)

Self-reference is given its most intense expression in his plea for personal liberty, a liberty going beyond the bounds of poetry to consider the poet as citizen (261-64). Although not phrased in the impartial vocabulary of the more theoretical statements, such passages represent the main thrust of the poem: the good poet is a dignified citizen whose restraint should be internally, and not externally, imposed. Poetry is a profession, practiced by the upright citizen, but not representing his sole activity or purpose in life.

Two theoretical passages in the "Epistle" are more aesthetically oriented. The qualities of a good poet are enumerated in the beginning of the attack on Atticus:

> ...but were there One whose fires
> True Genius kindles, and fair Fame inspires;
> Blest with each talent and each art to please,
> And born to write, converse, and live with ease.
> (193-96)

Besides providing a parallel to Horace's and Boileau's statements on genius and talent, the passage is similar to an earlier statement in the Essay on Criticism (48-49). Both describe the mental abilities and talents necessary for the task of good writing. Good poets are born and not made, though innate ability needs instruction. Truth also plays an important role in the aim of the poet, in the content of his verse and its style (334-43). Untainted by the transitory follies that debase poetry, the poet pleases by "manly ways," recalling the *virtus* (virtue) of the *vir bonus*. Not dazzled by the vagaries of "Fancy," the good poet aims for Truth and Virtue; the same standard maintained in the Essay on Criticism (562-63). With Truth as a poetic goal, it is not surprising that so much poetic advice in the "Epistle" tends toward the ethical.

In "To Mr. Fortescue" the persona presents himself as a plain, honest poet:

> I love to pour out all myself as plain
> As downright SHIPPEN, or as old MONTAIGNE:
> In them as certain to be loved as seen,
> The Soul stood forth, nor kept a thought within.
> (51-54)

He makes a playful, generic distinction of satire at the end of this text. Descriptions of genres have so far been absent from Pope's Imitations, in sharp contrast to their frequency in Boileau's Satires. Since the Essay on Criticism provides no discussion of satire as a genre, this passage is one of the few versified accounts of it in Pope's work:

> Libels and satires! lawless things indeed!
> But grave Epistles, bringing Vice to light,
> Such as a King might read, a Bishop write,
> Such as Sir ROBERT would approve ....
> (150-53)

But the generic distinction is not very detailed, and in fact most theoretical sections of Pope's satires are rarely developed. There is good reason for this. Since he wrote his poem on literary theory before his satires (unlike Horace and

Boileau), much of the theoretical base in the satires was a restatement of an earlier text. Turning to the Essay on Criticism, we can see Pope's first attempts at satire.

The satirical passages extend from the introductory lines to the final praise of Walsh. Although closer to Boileau's techniques and themes, the satire in the Essay is not as direct, personal, or ethically oriented as that in the Art poétique. Instead, it is directed more toward the improper mentality of authors. The usual victim is the vague substantive "Some" (26, 36, 289). Boileau's verve for "naming names" is absent. But the Essay appears more decorous because of the vague accusations. One person, however, provokes direct attacks: John Dennis (269-70, 584-89). The criticism of Dennis ends with the concept of dullness, one of the frequent charges of the satirist in the Essay. The cardinal vice of the Dunciad, dullness, is first attacked in the Essay (115, 358, 597, 608). It is readily apparent in a work, marking failure of the author to have mastered his craft effectively. No writer intends to be dull, so that such a writer is a ready-made target for satire.

Allusions to nonsense in the Essay are particularly important, focusing on the reverse of a major poetic standard of reasonable, good sense. The term occurs frequently as the criterion used to satirize a writer:

> In search of wit, these lose their common sense,
> And then turn critics in their own defense ....
> (28-29)
>
> These leave the sense, their learning to display,
> And those explain the meaning quite away.
> (116-17)

The standard of sense forms one of the positive goals used to measure the dull nonsense of bad poets.

Unlike the Ars poetica or the Art poétique, the Essay on Criticism often uses sexual allusions and innuendoes to ridicule bad writers. An ineffective writer becomes an ineffective lover, whose impotence is emblematic of a general worthlessness. Impotence itself is mentioned (533, 609), and eunuchs are evoked (31). Poetic infertility passes into unnatural fertility:

> Some neither can for wits nor critics pass,
> As heavy mules are neither horse, nor ass.
> Those half-learned witlings, num'rous in our isle,
> As half-formed insects on the banks of Nile;
> Unfinished things, one knows not what to call,
> Their generation's so equivocal ....
>
> (38-43)

Besides sexual humiliation, the satiric device of dehumanization is used frequently in the Essay. Satire demotes its victims by emphasizing faults and deficiencies. This has already been found in the *poetae insani* of Horace, and the *fats* and *sots* (fools) of Boileau. But only in the final passage of the Ars poetica, with the bad poet compared to a *hirudo* (leech), does one approach the level of dehumanization seen in the Essay. As we have seen, some authors are compared to mules and insects, in a kind of satiric metamorphosis as old as Simonides. Others are compared to moths and apes (112-13, 331-32). This technique creates vivid images, while providing one of the more drastic tactics of satire. The victim is no longer himself, but an animal, even an object.

A variety of satiric techniques occur frequently in the Essay on Criticism. Ethical in intention, they condemn poets for moral and social faults rather than specifically poetic, doctrinal deviations. The effect is stronger and more readily apprehended, as the satiric tone informs the most potent, expressive, and entertaining passages in the poem. It balances the dogmatic tone of the theory, showing the ridiculous shortcomings of those who fall far from the sublime ideal.

Satirical passages in the Arts of Poetry and theory in

the satires create a vital unity of thought and expression. Satires are justified and elevated by an overt standard of excellence, while the theoretical poems are enlivened and particularized with satiric examples. But differences in frequency and methodology attest to the individual talent of each of the three poets. Although they share a similar practice of combining satire and theory, none of the poets is a mere imitator.

The literary satires of Horace are especially noteworthy for their general aesthetic theory, presenting a more thorough and strictly poetic theory than the satires of Boileau and Pope. Ethics is important in these satires, but the high standards of the persona are stressed, not the faults of the satiric victims. In the Ars poetica, we find fewer satiric passages than in the Art poétique or Essay on Criticism, but they are used to greater structural effect (as a frame). A mad, disordered painter introduces the poem, and mad poets appear in the middle section and at the conclusion.

In Boileau's literary satires, theory is more limited, with the most extensive passages devoted to the genre of satire. And satire in the Art poétique is more frequent and direct than in the other theory poems. Pope's satires discuss more general theory, with Virtue being more of a standard than the Horatian *scribendi recte* (writing properly). Emphasis is placed on the poet rather than the poem. In contrast, when vice is presented in the Essay, the satire is less specific (the victim is "some"), but more sexual, base, or cruel.

The differences among the three poets indicate a variety of possibilities within a larger, unified tradition of writing literary satire and theoretical poems. Theory contributes to the content of the satires, and satire adds life to the theoretical poems; the inclusion of both extremes of good and bad poetic practice provides a necessary balance. Comparing both forms of poetry, their content is similar, with a shift in focus and in the role of the persona marking the different structural strategies. Originating from a single position of the poet evaluating the art of poetry, the two forms reveal the theoretical heights and the satiric lowlands of Mount Parnassus.

CHAPTER VII

CONCLUSION

All Bedlam, or Parnassus, is let out.
("Arbuthnot," 4)

One recurrent image which has appeared, in both a serious and an ironic context, is the mythological representation of Mount Parnassus. Situated in central Greece, the twin-peaked mountain has been associated with poets and poetry since the time of Hesiod. The simple, clear image of a mountain symbolizing a vertical hierarchy of poetic values figures prominently in the literary satires and the _Arts of Poetry_ of the three poets, as well as in this study. But the symbol itself is more complex than it might first appear, and it summarizes a more general mythology of poetic creation expressed in the poems we have examined.

Parnassus does imply a critical discrimination, with excellence located at the summit and failure at the bottom. The mountain functions as a metaphor, illustrating the difficulty of poetic craftsmanship in terms used to describe mountain climbing. The gravity of dullness and negligence always weighs heavily upon the aspiring poet, and causes many to fall. A dramatic and vivid quality in the mountain imagery maintains an entertaining aspect of the poems, while it also furthers the didactic intent. The term "Parnassus" also represents both the goal and the process for achieving it; the mountain is more than a static hierarchy, since it implies the dynamic movement of rising and falling poetic careers. Referring to more than the summit, the image also refers to the path leading toward it.

To explain different aspects of poetry, other mythological features expand the image of Parnassus. Apollo presides, and the nine Muses reside there. Pegasus often carries authors on poetic flights. All these names appear in the poems we have discussed, contributing symbolic insight into the general myth of native talent and inspiration. If we examine the ways in which each poet uses the different elements of the myth, we will arrive at a better understanding of its function.

Very few references to any aspect of the Parnassian myth exist in the literary satires or the Ars poetica of Horace. The Sermones are devoid of it, and only a few passages in the Ars poetica are pertinent to our discussion, as Horace appears to keep the focus of his work closely fixed on the human level of poetic craftsmanship. Only in explaining unknown phenomena, such as the rise of poetry in Greece, does he refer to mythology, "musa dedit fidibus divos puerosque deorum" (To the lyre the Muse granted tales of gods and children of the gods, 83). Parnassus itself is never mentioned in the Ars poetica. It is, therefore, not a Horatian topic. Mount Aetna serves an opposite function, though, demonstrating the folly of the suicidal Empedocles. The few references to the Muses, Helicon, and Apollo all occur in serious contexts, without any implication of irony or satire.

In the poetry of Boileau and Pope, however, the ironic tone is quite common. In Boileau's Satire IX the *je* asks his *Esprit* tauntingly, "Phébus a-t-il pour vous applani le Parnasse?" (Has Apollo flattened Parnassus for you?, 24), and Halifax is satirized in Pope's "Arbuthnot":

> Proud as Apollo on his forkèd hill
> Sat full-blown Bufo, puffed by every quill ....
> (231-32)

The change in tone between Horace and the later satirists can be attributed to each poet's taste, and the change in audience. One significant reason for both the ironic tone and the greater frequency of references lies in the use of Parnassus as a symbol in sixteenth and seventeenth century European literature. It had appeared in Dante (Purgatorio) and the Canterbury Tales ("Franklin's Prologue"). Occasional references occur through the fourteenth and fifteenth centuries, but it was not until the enormous success of Cesaro Caporali's satiric Viaggio al Parnasso (Voyage to Parnassus, 1580) that the image of Parnassus received widespread attention, especially as an extensive and ironic metaphor.[1]

In studying the image of Parnassus in Boileau and Pope, we should also notice that it is one of the few myths in the poems. Their content is oriented toward the actual situation of poetic practice, with many realistic references. But the myth provides a totally different context for considering and evaluating poetry. While much of the elaborate mythology of Renaissance poetry was removed from neoclassical verse, the Parnassus myth persisted. It figures prominently in the work of both Boileau and Pope and is a significant aspect of their poetry.

With Boileau, the myth of Parnassus is used extensively. Satire VII is addressed to the persona's Muse, while a description of the route to Parnassus forms the introductory passage of the Art poétique. The Muse is the most frequently used element in the myth, implying the quintessential *moi poétique*, the basic standard of poetic worth for the persona. In the satires the persona may be fallible, but this is not true for his Muse, who provides one of the means of the persona's credibility. He is inspired, and therein lies one value of his verse.

In the mythological complex of images, Apollo represents the supreme authority and poetic sanction, whose name is used more sparingly than that of the Muse. In Satire II the poetic mastery of Molière is expressed in terms of Apollo's special treatment of the dramatist, and in Satire VII the persona reclaims his role of poet because Apollo assists him. When a poet is favored by Apollo, there can be no further dispute, since the god of light, prophesy, and poetry is the ultimate arbiter of poets and their position on the mountain.

In Boileau, references to Parnassus occur in several different contexts, which extend the range of meaning of the image. The most general context relates to all poets, to a Republic of Letters. Boileau explains the events surrounding the publication of the Satires by referring to the community of all poets on Parnassus:

> ...je m'étais bien préparé au tumulte que l'impression de mon livre a excité sur le Parnasse.
> ("Discours sur la satire")

> I had been prepared for the tumult which the printing of my book aroused on Parnassus.

In the Art poétique he describes the development of French poetry using a nationalistic limitation to the term, alluding to a "Parnasse français" (I, 113). In both instances, good and bad poets are united in a general consideration of the entire mountain.

Other contexts emphasize only one extreme of Parnassus, either with a serious or ironic tone. The summit, and the excellent poets who finally arrive there, are mentioned seriously in Satire IX (279-82). Yet most of the references to Parnassus are ironic in this satire, since the *je* claims that his *Esprit* is presumptuous, and not worthy of a high position. Throughout the poetry of Boileau, the ironic context often found with this image indicates a poet's shortcomings, and the abuses the standard of excellence must suffer from the numerous bad poets. Finally, we have the bottom of Parnassus. In the beginning of the Art poétique, a bold but untalented author is unable to rise. In Satire IX a group of bad poets is ridiculed, "Je crains peu, direz-vous, les Braves du Parnasse" ("I hardly fear, you say, the dandies of Parnassus," 320). The image of Parnassus is both rich in implications and subtle in the nuances of its use throughout Boileau's poetry.

With Pope, we see fewer references to the various elements of the myth, yet they are nonetheless important. Pope also speaks of "my Muse" ("Fortescue," 57), and refers to himself by this title at the end of the Essay. Apollo is rarely named, except in the ironic context in which Bufo is satirized. Irony predominates in many of the references to Parnassus itself, as the standard of excellence is devalued amongst bad poets and critics:

> Whom have I hurt? has poet yet, or Peer,
> Lost the arched eyebrow, or Parnassian sneer?
> ("Arbuthnot," 95-96)

But there is still hope, and an occasional passage in which the sanctity of the mountain is maintained. The model of Greek poetry demonstrated the same high seriousness of poetry which the persona in the Essay conveys:

> High on Parnassus' top her sons she showed,
> And pointed out those arduous paths they trod;
> Held from afar, aloft, th'immortal prize,
> And urged the rest by equal steps to rise.
> (94-97)

This is the mission of all three poets, who use the myth of Parnassus to reveal both the heights of poetic excellence and the depths of failure as two extremes of the same hierarchy. Despite the vast separation between good and bad poets, a unity of vision is maintained as the poets represent poetic activity, its process and results, with the single image of Mount Parnassus.

We have examined the relationship between the literary satires and the poems of literary theory of Horace, Boileau, and Pope, and discovered that formal, structural differences exist, but so too does a similarity of content, tone, and focus (based upon writing). Both provide a critical, analytical survey of contemporary poetry, and contain a personal exposition of the poet's evaluations of literary practices.

Numerous examples of good and bad poets clarify the theoretical passages in each poem. Yet this material is organized in different ways, as each form establishes a distinct fictional framework in order to move the reader to a different persuasive end.

The texts we have examined are often considered to be structureless, or at least to contain problematic structures. In this study we have demonstrated the presence of a plot in the literary satires, and a pattern of alternations in the *Arts of Poetry*, and we have explored reasons for these structures and explanations for their differences. Secondly, the important role of the poet's persona in both forms of poetry has clarified the nature of the fiction in them. Each of the three poets enjoyed a limited amount of freedom in portraying a relatively accurate figure of himself in his different poems -- truthful enough to pertain to his own polemical situation, yet fictive enough to be rhetorically effective.

Finally, we have seen how we as readers are engaged in the texts. Moved in different ways to separate goals, we are led to believe the poet by means of his persona and the structure of each poem. We accept with him that certain poets are good and others bad, that a certain set of criteria are justified for the proper evaluation of poetry. And we finally believe in him, as satirist and as critic. We are persuaded to his point of view, to his creation of a poetic hierarchy, and his ranking of poets on Mount Parnassus.

FOOTNOTES

Chapter 1:

1. Horace, *Ars poetica*, 38-40; Boileau, *Art poétique*, I, 11-14; and Pope, *An Essay on Criticism*, 52-53, 60-61. The editions to be used for the primary texts are Wickham for Horace, Boudhors for Boileau, and Croker for Pope (listed in the bibliography). I have modernized the spelling of the Boudhors' Boileau. Translations from Latin and French are mine.

2. Alvin Kernan, *The Plot of Satire* (New Haven, Yale University Press, 1965), 11.

3. C.O. Brink, *Horace on Poetry: Prolegomena to the Literary Epistles* (Cambridge: Cambridge University Press, 1963), 154.

4. Despite the abundance of criticism on satire within the last few decades, there has not been a study devoted to the particular form of literary satire. Such a study would need to provide a historical framework for the form, which the following list describes as a larger context for the present study. It covers the major texts, but is not exhaustive (nor does it extend beyond 1800).

Classical: Aristophanes *Frogs*; Callimachus *Iambi* (now mostly fragments); Horace *Sermones* 1.4, 1.10, 2.1; Persius *Satire* 1; Juvenal *Satire* 1; sections of Petronius *Satyricon*.

English: Chaucer ("Sir Thopas," "Nun's Priest's Tale"); Donne *Satire* II; the Poetemachia or War of the Theatres involving Joseph Hall *Virgidemiarum* I, 1, 2, 9, Marston *Scourge of Villanie*, Jonson *Poetaster*, and Dekker *Satiromastix*; sections of Jonson *Epicoene*; Buckingham *The Rehearsal*; Dryden *Mac Flecknoe*; Oldham *Satyr concerning poetry*; Prior *A Satyr upon the Poets*; Swift *Battle of the Books* and sections of *Gulliver's Travels*; Pope *Dunciad*, *Peri Bathous*, and *Imitations from Horace*; Sheridan *The Critic*.

French: Marot "Le Valet de Marot contre Sagon"; Rabelais *Pantagruel* (librairie de Saint Victor); DuBellay "Musagnoeomachie," "La Nouvelle manière de faire son profit des lettres," and "Le Poète courtisan"; Ronsard "Discours à Guillaume des Autels," and "Réponse aux Prédicants de Genève"; Vauquelin de la Fresnay "Si pour avoir tu suis la Poésie"; Régnier *Satires* IX and XII; Saint-Evremond *Comédie des Académistes*; Scarron *Virgile travesti*; Sarasin "La Défaite des Bouts Rimés"; Molière *Les Précieuses Ridicules* and *La Critique de l'Ecole des Femmes*; satires against Boileau by Boursault, Cotin, Regnard, Nevers; sections of La Bruyère *Les*

Caractères; Voltaire "Le Temple du Goût," and some Satires ("La Cabale").

5. Critical monographs focus on one specific author. Two dissertations deal with all three authors. Robert Dupree in Boileau and Pope: The Horatian Perspective in France and England (1967) gives a historical account of the reception and influence of the Horatian mode of poetry in France and England (treating each separately). Satires on literature do not figure prominently, nor is there a sustained analysis of textual structures. In Ronald Bogue's The Art of the Art of Poetry: Graceful Negligence and Structure in Horace's Ars poetica, Boileau's Art poétique and Pope's Essay on Criticism (1975) structural elements in the Arts of Poetry (but not the satires) are examined. The general pattern of *poesis/poema/poeta* (poetry/poem/poet) is explored, but emphasis is placed on the ordering (not unifying) principles in the texts and their style of "grace" and "negligence."

6. The influence of Boileau upon later satirists, including Pope, is considerable. As Howard D. Weinbrot writes in Alexander Pope and the Traditions of Formal Verse Satire (Princeton: Princeton University Press, 1982), 83:

> Boileau, I believe, is the man to whom we must turn for an early model of how to make a synthesized, modern, formal verse satire.

7. Jean Marmier, Horace en France, au dix-septième siècle (Paris: Presses Universitaires de France, 1962), 99.

8. Satire IX, 61-62. Boileau also acknowledged his debt to Horace at the end of the Art poétique:

> ...ces leçons que ma Muse au Parnasse
> Rapporta jeune encor du commerce d'Horace
> (IV, 227-28)
>
> ...these lessons, which my Muse on Parnassus
> Brought back to me, while still young, after dealing with Horace.

and in Epître 8:

> Horace tant de fois dans mes vers imité,
> (87)
>
> Horace, imitated so often in my verse,....

9. Caroline Goad, Horace in the English Literature of the Eighteenth Century (1918; rpt. New York: Haskell House Publishers, 1967), 130. The quotation from Pope comes from the Imitations from Horace, Second Epistle to the Second Book, 144.

10. Ronald Paulson, The Fictions of Satire (Baltimore: Johns Hopkins Press, 1967), 3.

11. Jules Brody, "Boileau et la critique poétique," CCL (see bibliography), 250.

12. Maynard Mack, "The Muse of Satire," Yale Review, 41 (1951), 83.

13. William F. Cunningham, Jr., "Symposium: The Concept of the Persona in Satire," Satire Newsletter, 3, 2 (Spring, 1966), 94.

14. Charles Churchill, "The Apology," *The Poetical Works of Charles Churchill*, ed. Douglas Grant (Oxford: Clarendon Press, 1956), 41.

Chapter 2:

1. Pope, "Dialogue II, Epilogue to the Satires," 246-47.
2. Patricia Meyer Spacks, *An Argument of Images: The Poetry of Alexander Pope* (Cambridge, Mass.: Harvard University Press, 1971), 176.
3. W.O.S. Sutherland Jr. discusses the symbolic fiction of names in relationship to Dryden's satire in *The Art of the Satirist: Essays on the Satire of Augustan England* (Austin: University of Texas Press, 1965), 19:

> The man Shaftesbury is immaterial. It is the values symbolized by the man that constitute the poet's object. The modern tends to think of Shaftesbury as a historical fact. ...Dryden and his contemporaries ... judged him by what he believed, by the values he held.... For Dryden, then, Shaftesbury is a symbol representing a complex of values rather than a human being.... Especially in personal, political, or literary satire it is accurate to say that the "object" of satire is actually a symbol. The author is at bottom attacking a set of inimical values.

4. A name is needed for the satiric victim -- whether general or specific -- for it to work. As Richard Morton points out in "Introduction: Satire and Reform" in *Satire in the 18th Century*, J.D. Browning ed. (New York: Garland, 1982),2:

> ...without his own name attached, no reader, however foppish, avaricious or venal, will see himself in the satiric mirror. Satire, almost by definition, is about other people; the person attacked is an assumed, rather than an actual reader.

5. On the relation of satire to reality, Bernard Beugnot states in "Boileau et la distance critique," *Etudes françaises*, 5 (mai, 1969), 198:

> La satire pourrait se définir comme une poésie de la distance: ...elle coupe les liens de l'habitude et de la complaisance, elle sépare et disjoint ....
>
> Satire could be defined as a poetry of distance: it cuts the bonds of habit and complacency, it separates and breaks up ....

As for a correction of history, A. Kibédi-Varga states in "La Vraisemblance -- problèmes de terminologie, problèmes de poétique," *CCL*, 328:

L'histoire est injuste, elle "fait aussi bien prospérer les méchants que les bons"; notre conscience morale exige qu'elle soit corrigée. Voilà la tâche de la poésie, la vraisemblance est nécessaire afin que la poésie puisse atteindre son but, "l'amendement" des moeurs.

History is unjust, it "makes the evil prosper as well as the good;" our moral conscience demands that it be corrected. That is the task of poetry, plausibility is necessary so that poetry can attain its goal, "correcting" morals.

6. E.B.O. Borgerhoff, "Boileau Satirist *animi gratia*," Romanic Review, 43 (1952), 245.

7. Émile Benveniste, Problèmes de linguistique générale, (Paris: Gallimard, 1966), 252.

8. "Il nous est tombé du ciel un nouveau Caton le Censeur, qui encourage de sa verve un censeur triste et sévère," (A new Cato the Censor has fallen from the sky, who encourages by his verve a poor, severe censor), from Charles Cotin's La Critique désintéressée sur les Satyres du temps. See Boudhors, vol. 1, 265, note to verse 8.

9. Antoine Adam, Les Premières Satires de Boileau (1941; rpt. Genève: Slatkine Reprints, 1970), 34.

10. Tzvetan Todorov, "Introduction," Communications, 11 (1968), 1.

11. This view of the satiric *leçon* as an exercise in *vraisemblance* finds support in a passage by Todorov concerning two disputants delivering their differing *récits*:

> ...il ne s'agit plus d'établir une vérité (ce qui est impossible) mais de l'approcher, d'en donner l'impression; et cette impression sera d'autant plus forte que le récit sera plus habile. Pour gagner le procès, il importe moins d'avoir bien agi que de bien parler. Platon écrira "...la persuasion relève de la vraisemblance."
>
> It is no longer a matter of establishing the truth (which is impossible) but of approaching it, of giving an impression of it; and this impression will be that much stronger when the account is more skillful. To win the case, it matters less to have acted well, than to have spoken well. Plato supposedly wrote "persuasion springs from plausibility."

This is found on the same page as the previous note.

Chapter 3:

1. The traditional view of formal verse satire, which for modern criticism rests upon Mary Claire Randolph's "The Structural Design of the Formal Verse Satire," Philological

Quarterly (1942), places a two part structure in the poem: a vice is exposed to ridicule, followed by the virtue which is recommended.

2. Alvin Kernan, The Cankered Muse (New Haven: Yale University Press, 1959), 30.

3. In The Plot of Satire, Kernan concedes that "satire never offers that direct, linear progression which is ordinarily taken as plot" (100), but he does find patterns and plot movements in The Dunciad (all or nothing), Volpone, (rising and falling), and the novels of Evelyn Waugh (running in circles). He does not trace a plot for formal verse satire.

4. See, for example, Frankel p. 126, Brink I pp. 161-63, Fiske p. 277. These works represent major contributions to the view of the bipartite structure of the work.

5. Obviously the potential for a pun on the French homophones *les vers* (worms) and *les vers* (verses) is not lost upon Boileau who uses both words as end rhymes in this poem. There is no clear pun intended, however, in this passage.

6. The image of the *étamine* or filter is not only a topic of French satire, found in Régnier's Satire XIV (4), but is an important image in Montaigne ("De l'Institution des Enfants").

7. This poem was the second satire which Boileau wrote, finished three years before the first published edition of the Satires in 1666.

Chapter 4:

1. For the concept of a "friendly enemy," see Susan W. Tiefenbrun, "Boileau and his Friendly Enemy: A Poetics of Satiric Criticism," Modern Language Notes, 91,4 (May, 1976), 672-697.

2. There have been innumerable laws against satire, going back all the way to the Twelve Tables of Roman law. The fragment from Tabula 8, number 1, enumerating capital offenses, begins "Qui malum carmen incantassit" (Who sings evil songs). For greater details, see Textes de Droit Romain, annotés par Paul Frédéric Girard (Paris: Arthur Rousseau, 1890), 16.

3. The alternative genre is not always panegyric. This can be seen most clearly in Boileau's Satire IX, where the persona questions himself on the suitability of undertaking the ode, or the eclogue (250-260).

4. Dustin Griffin points out in Alexander Pope: The Poet in the Poems (Princeton: Princeton University Press, 1978), 165, concerning the Horatian Imitations, that:

> Studying his own character and experience provides him a focus for exploring the kinds of moral

> and psychological demands and predicaments that confront all those who, like himself, must live in a world at once exhilirating, gratifying, and offensive.

5. The satirist often uses an egalitarian tactic as one of his defenses. The persona in Sermo 2.1 describes far more despicable pastimes which other people are allowed, while he is constrained not to write satire. In Satire IX, Boileau speaks of the critical freedom of "every fool and knave," and then asks the rhetorical questions:

> Et je serai le seul qui ne pourrai rien dire?
> On sera ridicule, et je n'oserai rire?
> (191-192)
>
> And I will be the only one who can say nothing?
> People will be fools, and I don't dare laugh?

All three poets argue that a greater injustice would be done if they were not allowed to write satire.

6. Although the satirists claim their verse is mild and modest, they speak of their satire as a necessary weapon of self-defense (Horace, Sermo 2.1, 39-41; Boileau's numerous references to "attack"; Pope, "Fortescue," 69-72).

7. Edward A. Bloom and Lillian D. Bloom write in Satire's Persuasive Voice (Ithaca: Cornell University Press, 1979), 119:

> ...the satirist must be at the very least the forthright judge who will induce others to sit on the bench with him and share his rulings on matters of truth and justice. And he must be the attorney whose briefs will effect a favorable outcome. Ultimately he must translate his criticism into literature.

Therefore, the "persuasive verbal pitch" is essential to satire.

Chapter 5:

1. The importance of roles and the "drama" of the poem are stressed by Gordon Pocock in Boileau and the Nature of Neo-Classicism (Cambridge: Cambridge University Press, 1980), 83:

> I will approach L'Art poétique from a different angle, and one more typical of recent criticism: from the consideration of the poem as a dramatic event.

2. The reactions are often stated in terms of personal taste, his own likes and dislikes. Two proscriptions are stated with the verb *haïr* (to hate), but the majority of personal preferences convey what the persona likes (*aimer*). Such a use of personal preferences varies the tone from the

dogmatic air of a treatise to a more friendly piece of advice.

3. The two most frequent imperatives are *soyez*, (be) implying a basic, unchanging state of existence (I, 101, 183; III, 257, 258; IV, 26, 122) and *aimez*, which advises a certain attitude or state of mind (I, 37, 141, 191; III, 307; IV, 59, 108). With both imperatives it is unclear whether the addressee already has these skills and attitudes, as the persona urges him to retain them, or whether the addressee must adopt new skills and attitudes. The result, nonetheless, will be the same; the addressee will follow all the advice implied by the imperatives.

4. As Brody states:

> *Aimez* et *Fuyez*, ses conseils caractéristiques, marquent les deux pôles de sa sensibilité littéraire.
>
> *Love* and *Flee*, his characteristic pieces of advice, indicate the two poles of his literary sensibility.

Jules Brody, "La Métaphore érotique dans la critique de Boileau," La Cohérence intérieure, Jacqueline Van Baelen et David L. Rubin, éds. (Paris: Jean-Michel Place, 1977), 232.

5. In An Argument of Images Patricia Meyer Spacks discusses this metamorphosis in the following terms:

> ...[Pope] returns to self-description, personifying himself as a muse. This is a daring way to end the poem, and an appropriate one. Pope himself becomes an image, as he was to do again in the Horatian imitations, and demonstrates, through his capacity to fictionalize in this way, his determination to embody the fusion of criticism, poetry, and morality that has been the ideal throughout the poem. (31)

6. An example of the numerous patterns and structuring devices which can be found in the Arts of Poetry is provided by criticism of the Essay on Criticism. Arthur Fenner speaks of a "moral cast" over the poem caused by allusions to folly, pride, and evil. Urging a unity of rhetoric, Harold F. De Lisle outlines the first section "in accordance with the traditional divisions of a classical oration;" while Martin Kallich argues that the rhetorical figure of the antithesis structures the poem. Patricia Meyer Spacks analyzes methodologically the total pattern of imagery. Concentrating more on specific images and the concept of "nature," John M. Aden observes the importance and frequency of the key term. Finally, the specific concept of "wit" is discussed by Edward Niles Hooker, who provides the historical context for Pope's defense of wit, and by William Empson, who distinguishes the various meanings of "wit" in the text. Indeed, all these structural strategies shape the form of the text, including an alternation between bad and good poetic practices. Com-

plete references for these works are found in the bibliography.

Chapter 6:

1. Although the terms *satura* and *sermo* (as the genre of satire) never appear in the Ars poetica, "satire" does appear in Boileau's Art poétique and Pope's Essay on Criticism.

2. Other passages indicating satiric laughter in the Ars poetica occur in the discussion of the decorum of matching words with action (104, 112) and in the discussion of poets who continue to make the same errors (355-358).

3. Nathan Edelman aptly states that "It is the poet-satirist that animates the critic in Boileau," in "L'Art poétique: 'Longtemps plaire, et jamais ne lasser,'" in Studies in Seventeenth Century French Literature Presented to Morris Bishop, Jean-Jacques Demorest, ed. (Ithaca: Cornell University Press, 1962), 231.

4. In those passages without names, the terms *rimeur*, *sot*, and *vain Auteur* refer sometimes to a specific author (as to Lope de Vega at III, 39), sometimes to no author in particular. Whether or not the Art poétique was a *satire à clef* is unknown, but the hypothesis appears unlikely, considering Boileau's customary frankness and the silence of his usually vocal opponents.

Chapter 7:

1. Several other works followed the example of the Viaggio: The Parnassus Plays (c. 1600), Boccalini's Ragguali di Parnaso (1612-13), and Cervantes' Viaje del Parnaso (1615).

BIBLIOGRAPHY

<u>Abbreviations</u>:

CCL = Critique et création littéraires en France au XVIIe siècle, éd. Marc Fumaroli, Centre National de la Recherche Scientifique, No. 557. Paris: Editions du Centre National de la Recherche Scientifique, 1977.

<u>Editions Used</u>:

Boileau-Despréaux, Nicolas. Art poétique dans Epîtres, Art poétique, Lutrin, éd. Charles-H. Boudhors. Paris: Société les Belles Lettres, 1952, t. II.

----------. Les Satires, éd. Charles-H. Boudhors. Paris: Société les Belles Lettres, 1952, t. I.

Quintus Horatius Flaccus. Opera, ed. Edward C. Wickham. 1901; rpt. Oxford: Clarendon Press, 1967.

Pope, Alexander. The Works of Alexander Pope, eds. John Wilson Croker, Whitwell Elwin, and William John Courthope. 1871-1886; rpt. New York: Gordian Press, 1967.

<u>General Reference</u>

Adam, Antoine. Histoire de la littérature française au XVIIe siècle. 5 tomes. Paris: Domat, 1949-1954.

Atkins, J.W.H. Literary Criticism in Antiquity: A Sketch of Its Development. 2 vols. 1934; rpt. Gloucester, Mass.: Peter Smith, 1961.

Benveniste, Emile. Problèmes de linguistique générale. Paris: Gallimard, 1966.

Bogue, Ronald. "The Art of the Art of Poetry: Graceful Negligence and Structure in Horace's Ars Poetica, Boileau's Art poétique, and Pope's Essay on Criticism." Diss. University of Oregon, 1975.

Borgerhoff, E.B.O. The Freedom of French Classicism. Princeton: Princeton University Press, 1950.

Bray, René. La Formation de la doctrine classique en France. 1927; rpt. Paris: Nizet, 1966.

Bullough, Edward. "'Psychical Distance' as a Factor in Art and an Aesthetic Principle." British Journal of Psychology, 5 (1912), 87-118.

Churchill, Charles. The Poetical Works of Charles Churchill, ed. Douglas Grant. Oxford: Clarendon Press, 1956.

Cicero, Marcus Tullius. Orator, ed. H.M. Hubbell. 1939;

rpt. Cambridge, Mass.: Harvard University Press, 1962.

Clark, A.F.B. Boileau and the French Classical Critics in England. Paris: Champion, 1925.

Cook, A.S. The Art of Poetry: The Poetical Treatises of Horace, Vida, and Boileau. Boston: Ginn and Co., 1892.

Dryden, John. Essays of John Dryden, ed. W.P. Ker. 2 vols. Oxford: Clarendon Press, 1900.

Dupree, Robert. "Boileau and Pope: The Horatian Perspective in France and England." Diss. Yale University, 1966.

Ehrenpreis, Irvin. "Personae," Restoration and Eighteenth Century Literature, ed. Charles Carroll Camden. Chicago: University of Chicago Press, 1963.

Fleuret, Fernand et Louis Perceau. Les Satires françaises du XVIIe siècle. 2 tomes. Paris: Garnier, 1923.

Genette, Gérard. "Vraisemblance et motivation," Communications, 11 (1968), 4-11.

Grube, G.M.A. The Greek and Roman Critics. Toronto: University of Toronto Press, 1965.

Highet, Gilbert. The Classical Tradition: Greek and Roman Influences on Western Literature. London: Oxford University Press, 1949.

Huizinga, Johan. Homo Ludens. London: Routledge and K. Paul, 1949.

Jolles, André. Einfache Formen. 1930; rpt. Tübingen: M. Niemeyer, 1972.

Kibédi-Varga, A. "La Vraisemblance -- problèmes de terminologie, problèmes de poétique," CCL, 325-332.

Leeman, A.D. "Horace et Boileau: étude comparative," CCL, 1-6.

Marmier, Jean. "La Conscience du satirique, d'Horace à Boileau," CCL, 29-37.

Spingarn, J.E., ed. Critical Essays of the Seventeenth Century. 3 vols. Oxford: Clarendon Press, 1908.

Tayler, Edward W. Literary Criticism of Seventeenth Century England. New York: Alfred A. Knopf, 1967.

Textes de Droit Romain, annotés Paul Frédéric Girard. Paris: Arthur Rousseau, 1890.

Tillotson, Geoffrey. "Pope and Boileau," Notes and Queries, 205 (1960), 294.

Todorov, Tzvetan. "Introduction," Communications, 11 (1968), 1-3.

Voltaire. "Art poétique" dans Dictionnaire philosophique, éd. Benchot (Paris: Garnier, 1878), XVII, 430-432.

Weinbrot, Howard D. "The Pattern of Formal Verse Satire in the Restoration and the Eighteenth Century," PMLA, 80 (1965), 394-401.

Weinberg, Bernard. A History of Literary Criticism in the Italian Renaissance. 2 vols. Chicago: University of Chicago Press, 1961.

Wright, George T. The Poet in the Poem: The Personae of Eliot, Yeats, and Pound. Berkeley: University of California Press, 1960.

Works on Satire

Booth, Wayne. *A Rhetoric of Irony*. Chicago: University of Chicago Press, 1974.

Bloom, Edward A. and Lillian D. *Satire's Persuasive Voice*. Ithaca: Cornell University Press, 1979.

----------. "The Satiric Mode of Feeling: A Theory of Intention," *Criticism*, 11 (1969), 115-139.

Bredvold, Louis I. "A Note in Defense of Satire," *Journal of English Literary History*, 7 (1940), 253-264.

Brilli, Attilio. *Retorica della satira*. Bologna: Società editrice il Mulino, 1973.

Browning, J.D., ed. *Satire in the 18th Century*. New York: Garland, 1983.

Cunningham, William F. Jr. "Symposium: The Concept of the Persona in Satire," *Satire Newsletter*, 3,2 (1966), 92-95.

Ehrenpreis, Irvin. "The Literary Side of a Satirist's Work," *Minnesota Review*, II,2 (1962), 179-197.

Elkin, P.K. *The Augustan Defence of Satire.* Oxford: Clarendon Press, 1973.

Elliott, Robert C. *The Power of Satire: Magic, Ritual, Art*. Princeton: Princeton University Press, 1960.

Feinberg, Leonard. *Introduction to Satire*. Ames, Iowa: Iowa State University Press, 1967.

----------. *The Satirist*. Ames, Iowa: Iowa State University Press, 1963.

Frye, Northrup. "The Mythos of Winter: Irony and Satire," *The Anatomy of Criticism*. Princeton: Princeton University Press, 1957, 223-239.

----------. "The Nature of Satire," *University of Toronto Quarterly*, 14 (1944), 75-89.

Highet, Gilbert. *The Anatomy of Satire*. Princeton: Princeton University Press, 1962.

Hodgart, Matthew. *Satire*. New York: McGraw-Hill, World University Library, 1969.

Jack, Ian. *Augustan Satire: Intention and Idiom in English Poetry 1660-1750*. Oxford: Clarendon Press, 1952.

Jensen, H. James and Malvin R. Zirker, Jr. eds. *The Satirist's Art*. Bloomington: Indiana University Press, 1972.

Kernan, Alvin. *The Cankered Muse: Satire of the English Renaissance*. New Haven: Yale University Press, 1959.

----------. *The Plot of Satire*. New Haven: Yale University Press, 1965.

Knox, E.V. *The Mechanism of Satire*. Cambridge: Cambridge University Press, 1951.

Limentani, Uberto. *La Satira nel Seicento*. Milano: Riccardo Ricciardi, 1961.

Mack, Maynard. "The Muse of Satire," Yale Review, 49 (1951), 80-92.
----------, ed. Satire: Modern Essays in Criticism. Englewood Cliffs, N.J.: Prentice-Hall, 1971.
Nichols, James W. Insinuation: The Tactics of English Satire. The Hague: Mouton, 1971.
"The Norms in Satire: A Symposium," Satire Newsletter, 2,1 (1964), 4-26.
Paulson, Ronald. The Fictions of Satire. Baltimore: Johns Hopkins Press, 1967.
Powers, Doris C. English Formal Satire. The Hague: Mouton, 1971.
Randolph, Mary Claire. "The Structural Design of the Formal Verse Satire," Philological Quarterly, 21 (1942), 368-384.
Satire Newsletter, (1963-1973).
Shero, L.R. "The Satirist's Apologia," University of Wisconsin Studies, 15 (1922), 148-167.
Sutherland, James. English Satire. Cambridge: Cambridge University Press, 1958.
Sutherland, W.O.S. Jr. The Art of the Satirist. Austin: University of Texas Press, 1965.
"Symposium: The Concept of the Persona in Satire," Satire Newsletter, 3,2 (1966), 89-153.
Trickett, Rachel. The Honest Muse: A Study in Augustan Verse. Oxford: Clarendon Press, 1967.
Van Rooy, Charles August. Studies in Classical Satire and Related Literary Theory. Leiden: E.J. Brill, 1966.
Williamson, George. "The Rhetorical Pattern of Neo-classical Wit," Modern Philology, 33 (1935), 58-81.
Witke, Charles. Latin Satire: The Structure of Persuasion. Leiden: E.J. Brill, 1970.
Worcester, David. The Art of Satire. Cambridge, Mass: Harvard University Press, 1940.

Works on Horace

Anderson, William S. Essays on Roman Satire. Princeton: Princeton University Press, 1982.
Bailey, D.R. Shackleton. Profile of Horace. Cambridge, Mass.: Harvard University Press, 1982.
Becker, Carl. Das Spätwerk des Horaz. Göttingen: Vandenhoeck und Ruprecht, 1963.
Brink, C.O. Horace on Poetry,I: Prolegomena to the Literary Epistles. Cambridge: Cambridge University Press, 1963.
----------. Horace on Poetry, II: The Ars Poetica. Cambridge: Cambridge University Press, 1971.
Campbell, Archibald Young. Horace: A New Interpretation. London: Methuen and Co., 1924.

Cartault, A. Etude sur les Satires d'Horace. Bibliothèque de la Faculté des Lettres, No. 9. Paris: Germer Baillière, 1899.

Cauer, Paul. "Zur Abgrenzung und Verbildung der Teile in Horazens Ars Poetica." Rheinisches Museum, 61 (1906), 232-243.

Coffey, Michael. Roman Satire. London: Methuen, 1976.

Cooper, Lane ed. A Concordance to the Works of Horace. Carnegie Institute of Washington, No. 202. Washington, D.C.: Carnegie Institute, 1916.

D'Alton, J.F. Roman Literary Theory and Criticism: A Study in Tendencies. 1931; rpt. New York: Russell and Russell, 1962.

Fairclough, H.R. "Horace's View of Relations Between Satire and Comedy," American Journal of Philology, 34 (1913), 183-193.

Fiske, G.C. Lucilius and Horace, A Study in the Classical Theory of Imitation. University of Wisconsin Studies, No. 7. Madison: University of Wisconsin Press, 1920.

Fiske, G.C. and Mary A. Grant. "Cicero's Orator and Horace's Ars Poetica," Harvard Studies in Classical Philology, 35 (1924), 1-74.

Fraenkel, Edward. Horace. Oxford: Clarendon Press, 1957.

Frank, Tenney. "Horace on Contemporary Poetry," Classical Journal, 13 (1917-1918), 550-564.

----------. "Horace's Definition of Poetry." Classical Journal, 31 (1935-1936), 167-174.

----------. "On Horace's Controversies with the New Poets," Classical Studies presented to E. Caps. Princeton: Princeton University Press, 1936.

Grimal, Pierre. Essai sur l'Art poétique d'Horace. Paris: Sedes, 1968.

Gueuning, L. "Horace et la poésie," Les Etudes Classiques, 4 (1935), 52-73.

Hack, R.K. "The Doctrine of Literary Forms," Harvard Studies in Classical Philology, 27 (1916), 1-65.

Haight, Elizabeth H. "The Lyre and the Whetstone: Horace Redivivus," Classical Philology, 41 (1946), 132-142.

----------. "Horace on Art, ut pictura poesis." Classical Journal, 47 (1952), 157-162, 201-203.

Hendrickson, G.L. "Are the Letters of Horace Satires?" American Journal of Philology, 18 (1897), 313-324.

----------. "Horace and Lucilius: A Study of Horace, Serm. 1.10," Studies in Honor of Basil L. Gildersleeve. Baltimore: Johns Hopkins Press, 1902, 151-168.

----------. "Horace Serm. 1.4: A Protest and a Programme," American Journal of Philology, 21 (1900), 121-142.

----------. "Satura -- The Genesis of a Literary Form," Classical Philology, 6 (1911), 129-143.

----------. "Satura Tota Nostra Est," Classical Philology, 22 (1927), 46-60.

Immisch, Otto. "Horazens Epistel über die Dichtkunst," Phil-

ologus, Suppl. 24, No. 3 (1932).
Knapp, C. "The Sceptical Assault on the Roman Tradition Concerning the Dramatic Satura," American Journal of Philology, 33 (1912), 125-148.
Knoche, Ulrich. Roman Satire, trans. Edwin S. Ramage. Bloomington: Indiana University Press, 1975.
Krenkel, W.A. "Horace's Approach to Satire," Arthusa, 5 (1972), 7-16.
McKay, A.G. and D.M. Shepherd. Roman Satire. London: Macmillan Education, 1976.
Meuli, K. "Altrömischer Maskenbrauch," Museum Helveticum, 12 (1955), 206-235.
Morris, E.P. "The Form of the Epistle in Horace," Yale Classical Studies, 2 (1931), 79-114.
Nettleship, H. "The Original Form of the Roman Satura," rpt. in Lecture and Essays, 2nd series, ed. F. Haverfield. Oxford: Clarendon, 1895, 24-43.
Norden, Eduard. "Die Composition und Litteraturgattung der Horazischen Epistula ad Pisones," Hermes, 40 (1905), 481-528.
Perret, Jacques. Horace. Paris: Hatier, 1959.
Rackham, Horace. "Horace, Sat. 1.4.7," Classical Review, 30 (1916), 224.
Ramage, Edwin S., David L. Sigsbee, and Sigmund C. Fredericks. Roman Satirists and their Satire. Park Ridge, N.J.: Noyes Press, 1974.
Reitzenstein, R. "Zur römischen Satire (2). Zu Horaz Sat i.10 und i.4," Hermes, 59 (1924), 11-22.
Rudd, N. "Had Horace Been Criticised? A Study of Serm. 1.4," American Journal of Philology, 76 (1955), 165-175.
----------. "Horace and Fannius. A Discussion of Two Passages in Horace Serm. 1.4," Hermathena, 87 (1956), 49-60.
----------. "Horace and the Origins of Satura," Phoenix, 14 (1960), 36-44.
----------. "Horace, Sermones II,i," Hermathena, 90 (1957), 47-53.
----------. "The Names in Horace's Satires," Classical Quarterly, 10 (1960), 161-178.
----------. "The Poet's Defense," Classical Quarterly, 49 (1955), 142-156.
----------. The Satires of Horace: A Study. Cambridge: Cambridge University Press, 1966.
Rudd, W.J.N. "Libertas and Facetus, with Special Reference to Horace Serm. I,4 and I,10," Mnemosyne, 4,10 (1957), 319-336.
Showerman, Grant. Horace and His Influence. Boston: Marshal Jones Co., 1922.
Stégen, G. Les Epîtres littéraires d'Horace. Namur: A. Wesmael-Charlier, 1958.
Steidle, Wolf. Studien zur Ars Poetica des Horaz. 1937; rpt. Hildesheim: Olms, 1967.

Tate, J. "Horace and the Moral Function of Poetry," Classical Quarterly, 22 (1928), 65-73.
Tracy, H.L. "Horace's Ars Poetica: A Systematic Argument," Greece and Rome, 17 (1948), 104-115.
Ullman, B.L. "Dramatic Satura," Classical Philology, 9 (1914), 1-23.
----------. "Horace on the Nature of Satire," Transactions ... of the American Philological Association, 48 (1917), 111-132.
----------. "Satura and Satire," Classical Philology, 8 (1913), 172-194.
Van Rooy, C.A. "Arrangement and Structure of Satires in Horace, Sermones, Book I, with more Special Reference to Satires 1-4," Acta Classica, 11 (1968), 38-72.
Wagenvoort, H. "Ludus Poeticus," Les Etudes Classiques, 4 (1935), 108-120.
Wheeler, A.L. "Satura as a Generic Term," Classical Philology, 7 (1912), 457-477.

Works on Boileau

Adam, Antoine. "Boileau," dans Histoire de la littérature française au dix-septième siècle. Paris: Domat, 1952, III, 66-155.
----------. Les Premières Satires de Boileau. 1941; rpt. Genève: Slatkine Reprints, 1970.
Ascoli, Georges. Boileau: Satires de I à IX. Paris: Centre de Documentation Universitaire, s.d.
Beugnot, Bernard. "Boileau et la distance critique," Etudes françaises, 5 (1969), 195-206.
----------. "Boileau, une esthétique de la lumière," Studi francesi, 44 (1971), 229-237.
Beugnot, Bernard et Roger Zuber. Boileau: Visages anciens, visages nouveaux. Montréal: Les Presses de l'Université de Montréal, 1973.
Borgerhoff, E.B.O. "Boileau Satirist *animi gratia*," Romanic Review, 43 (1952), 241-255.
Bray, René. Boileau: L'homme et l'oeuvre. Paris: Boivin, 1942.
Brody, Jules. Boileau and Longinus. Geneva: Droz, 1958.
----------. "Boileau et la critique poétique," CCL, 231-250.
----------. "La métaphore érotique dans la critique de Boileau," La Cohérence intérieure: Etudes sur la littérature française du XVIIe siècle, présentées en hommage à Judd D. Hubert, Jacqueline Van Baelen et David L. Rubin, éds. Paris: Jean Michel Place, 1977, 223- 233.
Brunetière, Ferdinand. "L'Esthétique de Boileau," Revue des Deux Mondes, 69 (June, 1889), 662-685.
Clarac, Pierre. Boileau. Paris: Hatier, 1964.

Davidson, Hugh M. "The Idea of Literary History in the *Art poétique* of Boileau," *Symposium*, 18 (Autumn, 1964), 264-272.

----------. "The Literary Arts of Longinus and Boileau," *Studies in the Seventeenth Century French Literature*, ed. Jean-Jacques Demorest. Ithaca: Cornell University Press, 1962, 247-264.

Delaporte, Victor. *L'Art poétique de Boileau, commenté par Boileau et par ses contemporains*. Lille: Desclée, de Brouwer, et Cie, 1888.

Edelman, Nathan. "L'Art poétique: 'Long-temps plaire, et jamais ne lasser,'" in *Studies in Seventeenth Century French Literature*, ed. Jean-Jacques Demorest. Ithaca: Cornell University Press, 1962, 231-246.

Grimal, Pierre. "Boileau et l'*Art poétique* d'Horace," *CCL*, 183-193.

Haley, Sister Marie Philip. *Racine and the "Art poétique" of Boileau*. Baltimore: Johns Hopkins Press, 1938.

Hall, Gaston. "Aspects esthétiques et religieux de la querelle des Anciens et des Modernes: Boileau et Desmarets de Saint-Sorlin," *CCL*, 213-220.

Hervier, Marcel. *L'Art poétique de Boileau: étude et analyse*. Paris: Mellottée, 1938.

Lanson, Gustave. *Boileau*. Paris: Hachette, 1892.

----------. "Boileau: poète réaliste," dans *Essais de méthode, de critique et d'histoire littéraire*, presentés par Henri Peyre. Paris: Hachette, 1965, 291-296.

Levy, Robert H. "Rationalism and Classical Humanism: Boileau's *Art of Poetry*," *Enlightenment Essays*, No. 2 (Summer, 1970), 84-94.

Magne, Emile. *Bibliographie générale des oeuvres de Nicolas Boileau-Despréaux*. 2 tomes. Paris: Giraud-Badin, 1929.

Marmier, Jean. *Horace en France, au dix-septième siècle*. Paris: Presses Universitaires de France, 1962.

Mason, H.A. "Hommage à M. Despréaux," *Cambridge Quarterly*, 3, 1 (Winter, 1967-68), 51-71.

Morillot, Paul. *Boileau*. Paris: Lecène, Oudin et Cie, 1894.

Mornet, Daniel. *Nicolas Boileau*. Paris: Calmann-Lévy, 1941.

Noss, Mary T. "The Personality of Boileau," *French Review*, 5 (1938), 399-409.

----------. *La Sensibilité de Boileau*. Paris: Gamber, 1932.

Orr, John. "Pour le commentaire linguistique de l'Art poétique," *Revue de linguistique romane*, 99-100 (1961), 337-353.

Pocock, Gordon. *Boileau and the Nature of Neo-Classicism*. Cambridge: Cambridge University Press, 1980. reviewed, Allen Wood, *Papers on French Seventeenth Century Literature*, 9, 17 (1982), 789-791.

Revillout, Charles. "La Légende de Boileau," *Revue des Langues Romanes*, 34 (1890), 449-502; 35 (1892), 524-72; 37 (1894), 59-114, 149-81, 197-215, 374-82, 443-56, 552-65; 38 (1895), 75-83, 127-34, 221-31, 255-68, 316-29.

Sainte-Beuve, Charles-Augustin. "Boileau I," dans Les Grands écrivains français, XVIIe siècle; Les poètes, annotées par Maurice Allem. Paris: Garnier, 1927, 210-231.
----------. "Boileau II," dans Les Grands écrivains français, XVIIe siècle; Les poètes, annotées par Maurice Allem. Paris: Garnier, 1927, 232-253.
Schulz-Buschhaus, Ulrich. "Honnête Homme und Poeta doctus -- Zum Verhaltnis von Boileaus und Menzinis poetologischen Lehrgedichten," Arcadia, 9 (1974), 113-133.
Teifenbrun, Susan W. "Boileau and his Friendly Enemy: A Poetics of Satiric Criticism," Modern Language Notes, 91, 4 (May, 1976), 672-697.
Tocanne, Bernard. "Boileau et l'épopée d'après l'Art poétique," CCL, 203-211.
Van Delft, Louis. "Sur le statut de la maxime au XVIIe siècle: esthétique et éthique dans l'Art poétique," Esprit créateur, 22,3 (1981), 39-45.
Venesoen, Christian. "L'Entretien sur le bel-esprit de Bouhours: source de l'Art poétique de Boileau," XVIIe siècle, 89 (1970), 23-45.
Vitanovic, Slobodan. "Le Problème du génie dans la poétique de Boileau," CCL, 195-201.
White, Julian Eugene, Jr. Nicolas Boileau. New York: Twayne (TWAS 91), 1969.
Wood, Allen G. "Les Noms placés dans les niches: Satires and Sermons," Papers on French Seventeenth Century Literature, 9, 16 (1982), 89-101.
Zdrojewska, Vera. Boileau. Brescia: La Scuola, 1948.

Works on Pope

Abbott, Edwin. A Concordance to the Works of Alexander Pope. 1875; rpt. New York: Kraus Reprint Corporation, 1965.
Aden, John M. "The Doctrinal Design of An Essay on Criticism," College English, 22 (1961), 311-315.
----------. "'First Follow Nature': Strategy and Stratification in An Essay on Criticism," Journal of English and German Philology, 55 (1956), 604-617.
----------. "Pope and the Receit to Make a Satire," Satire Newsletter, 5 (1967), 25-33.
----------. "Pope and the Satiric Adversary," Studies in English Literature, 1500-1900, 2 (1962), 267-286.
----------. Pope's Once and Future Kings: Satire and Politics in the Early Career. Knoxville, Tenn.: University of Tennessee Press, 1978.
----------. Something Like Horace: Studies in the Art and Allusion of Pope's Horatian Satires. Kingsport, Tenn.: Vanderbilt University Press, 1969.
Adler, Jacob H. "Balance in Pope's Essays," English Studies,

43 (1962), 457-467.

Atkins, G. Douglas. "Poetic Strategies in An Essay on Criticism, Lines 201-559," South Atlantic Bulletin, 44,4 (1978), 43-47.

Audra, E. L'Influence française dans l'oeuvre de Pope. Paris: Champion, 1931.

Barnard, John, ed. Pope: The Critical Heritage. London: Routledge and Kegan Paul, 1973.

Bishop, Carter R. "General Themes in Pope's Satires," West Virginia University Bulletin: Philological Papers, 6 (1949), 54-68.

Boyce, Benjamin. The Character-Sketches in Pope's Poems. Durham, N.C.: Duke University Press, 1962.

Brower, Reuben Arthur. Alexander Pope: The Poetry of Allusion. Oxford: Clarendon Press, 1959.

Brown, Wallace Cable. "Dramatic Tension in Neoclassical Satire," College English, 6 (1945), 263-269.

Chesterton, G.K. "Pope and the Art of Satire," Varied Types. New York: Dodd, Mead and Co., 1905.

De Lisle, Harold F. "Structure in Part I of Pope's Essay on Criticism," English Language Notes, 1 (1963), 14-17.

Dixon, Peter. "The Theme of Friendship in the Epistle to Dr. Arbuthnot," English Studies, 44 (1963), 191-197.

----------. The World of Pope's Satires. London: Methuen, 1968.

Edwards, Thomas R., Jr. "Heroic Folly: Pope's Satiric Identity," in In Defense of Reading, ed. Reuben Brower and Richard Poirier. New York: Dutton, 1962, 191-205.

----------. This Dark Estate: A Reading of Pope. Berkeley: University of California Press, 1963.

Empson, William. "Wit in the Essay on Criticism," in Essential Articles for the Study of Alexander Pope, ed. Maynard Mack, rev. and enl. Hamden, Conn.: Archon Books, 1968, 208-226.

Feder, Lillian. "Sermon or Satire: Pope's Definition of his Art," Studies in Criticism and Aesthetics, 1660-1800: Essays in Honor of Samuel Holt Monk, ed. Howard Anderson and John S. Shea. Minneapolis: University of Minnesota Press, 1967.

Fenner, Arthur, Jr. "The Unity of Pope's Essay on Criticism," Philological Quarterly, 39 (1960), 435-436.

Fogle, Richard Harter. "Metaphors of Organic Unity in Pope's Essay on Criticism," Tulane Studies in English, 13 (1963), 51-58.

Goad, Caroline Mabel. Horace in the English Literature of the Eighteenth Century. 1918; rpt. New York: Haskell House, 1967.

Gordon, I.R.F. A Preface to Pope. London: Longman, 1976.

Greany, Helen T. "Satiric Masks: Swift and Pope," Satire Newsletter, 3 (1966), 154-159.

Greene, Donald J. "Dramatic Texture in Pope," From Sensibility to Romanticism: Essays Presented to Frederick A.

Pottle, ed. Frederick W. Hilles and Harold Bloom. New York: Oxford University Press, 1965.
Griffin, Dustin H. *Alexander Pope: The Poet in the Poems*. Princeton: Princeton University Press, 1978.
Harrihan, V. "The Seeing Eye: A View of the Structure of *An Epistle to Dr. Arbuthnot*," *Journal of English Studies*, 2 (1979), 41-47.
Hooker, Edward Niles. "Pope on Wit: The *Essay on Criticism*," in *Essential Articles for the Study of Alexander Pope*, ed. Maynard Mack, rev. and enl. Hamden, Conn.: Archon Books, 1968, 185-226.
Hughes, Richard Edward. "Pope's *Imitations of Horace* and the Ethical Focus," *Modern Language Notes*, 71 (1956), 569-574.
Hunter, G.K. "The Romanticism of Pope's Horace," *Essays in Criticism*, 10 (1960), 390-404.
Hunter, J. Paul. "Satiric Apology as Satiric Instance: Pope's *Arbuthnot*," *Journal of English and Germanic Philology*, 68 (1969), 625-647.
Kallich, Martin. "Image and Theme in Pope's *Essay on Criticism*," *Ball State University Forum*, 8,3 (1967), 54-60.
----------. "Pegasus on the Seesaw: Balance and Antithesis in Pope's *Essay on Criticism*," *Tennessee Studies in Literature*, 12 (1967), 57-68.
Keener, Frederick M. *An Essay on Pope*. New York: Columbia University Press, 1974.
Knight, G. Wilson. *The Poetry of Pope: Laureate of Peace*. London: Routledge and Kegan Paul, 1955.
Kupersmith, William. "Pope, Horace and the Critics: Some Reconsiderations," *Arion*, 9 (1970), 205-219.
Levine, Jay Arnold. "The Status of the Verse Epistle Before Pope," *Studies in Philology*, 59 (1962), 658-684.
MacDonald, W.L. *Pope and his Critics: A Study in Eighteenth Century Personalities*. London: J.M. Dent and Sons, 1951.
MacKillop, I.D. "The Satirist in His Own Person," in *The Art of Alexander Pope*, ed. Howard Erskine-Hill and Anne Smith. New York: Barnes and Noble, 1978, 157-168.
Mack, Maynard. *The Augustans*, 2nd ed. Englewood Cliffs, N.J.: Prentice-Hall, 1950.
----------, ed. *Essential Articles for the Study of Alexander Pope*, rev. and enl. Hamden, Conn.: Archon Books, 1968.
---------- and James A. Winn, eds. *Pope: Recent Essays*. Hamden, Conn.: Archon Books, 1980.
----------. "'Wit and Poetry and Pope': Some Observations on His Imagery," in *Pope and His Contemporaries: Essays Presented to George Sherburn*, ed. James L. Clifford and Louis A. Landa. Oxford: Clarendon Press, 1949.
Maner, Martin. "Pope, Byron, and the Satiric Persona," *Studies in English Literature, 1500-1900*, 20 (1980), 557-573.

Maresca, Thomas E. "Pope's Defense of Satire: The First Satire of the Second Book of Horace, Imitated," Journal of English Literary History, 31 (1964), 366-394.

----------. Pope's Horatian Poems. Columbus: Ohio State University Press, 1966.

Marks, Emerson R. "Pope on Poetry and the Poet," Criticism, 12 (1970), 271-280.

Mengel, Elias F., Jr. "Patterns of Imagery in Pope's Arbuthnot," PMLA, 69 (1954), 189-197.

Monk, Samuel Holt. "A Grace Beyond the Reach of Art," in Essential Articles for the Study of Alexander Pope, ed. Maynard Mack, rev. and enl. Hamden, Conn.: Archon Books, 1968, 38-62.

Olson, Elder. "Rhetoric and the Appreciation of Pope," Modern Philology, 37 (1939), 13-35.

Parkin, Rebecca Price. "Alexander Pope's Use of the Implied Dramatic Speaker," College English, 11 (1949), 137-141.

Paulson, Ronald. "Satire, and Poetry, and Pope," in Pope: Recent Essays, ed. Maynard Mack and James A. Winn. Hamdem, Conn.: Archon Books, 1980, 45-62.

Piper, William B. "The Conversational Poetry of Pope," Studies in English Literature, 1500-1900, 10 (1970), 505-524.

Rogers, Robert W. The Major Satires of Alexander Pope. Illinois Studies in Language and Literature, vol. 40. Urbana: University of Illinois Press, 1955.

Russo, John P. Alexander Pope: Tradition and Identity. Cambridge, Mass.: Harvard University Press, 1972.

Sierenberg, Edwin. "Art's Own Reason in an Age of Enlightenment: Pope's Essay on Criticism," Enlightenment Essays, 1 (1970), 179-189.

Spacks, Patricia Meyer. An Argument of Images: The Poetry of Alexander Pope. Cambridge, Mass.: Harvard University Press, 1971.

----------. "Imagery and Method in An Essay on Criticism," PMLA, 85 (1970), 97-106.

Tillotson, Geoffrey. On the Poetry of Pope, rev. ed. Oxford: Clarendon Press, 1950.

Warren, Austin. Alexander Pope as Critic and Humanist. Princeton: Princeton University Press, 1929.

----------. "The Mask of Pope," Sewanee Review, 54 (1946), 19-33.

Weber, Harold. "The Comic and Tragic Satirist in Pope's Imitations of Horace," Papers on Language and Literature, 16 (1982), 65-80.

Weinbrot, Howard D. Alexander Pope and the Traditions of Formal Verse Satire. Princeton: Princeton University Press, 1982.

----------. The Formal Strain: Studies in Augustan Imitation and Satire. Chicago: University of Chicago Press, 1969.